Short Bike Rides™
in and around
San Francisco

Help Us Keep This Guide Up to Date

Every effort has been made by the author and editors to make this guide as accurate and useful as possible. Many things can change, however, after a guide is published—establishments close, phone numbers change, facilities come under new management, etc.

We would love to hear from you concerning your experiences with this guide and how you feel it could be made better and be kept up to date. While we may not be able to respond to all comments and suggestions, we'll take them to heart, and we'll also make certain to share them with the author. Please send your comments and suggestions to the following address:

The Globe Pequot Press
Reader Response/Editorial Department
P.O. Box 833
Old Saybrook, CT 06475

Or you may e-mail us at:

editorial@globe-pequot.com

Thanks for your input, and happy travels!

Short Bike Rides™ Series

Short Bike Rides™
in and around
San Francisco

Second Edition

by

Henry Kingman

Old Saybrook, Connecticut

The information in the appendix (pp. 192–94) is reprinted, with permission, from RIDES for Bay Area Commuters. Special thanks to Carolyn Helmke.

Short Bike Rides is a trademark of The Globe Pequot Press, Inc.
Cover photo: Chris Dubé
Cover design: Saralyn D'Amato-Twomey

All photographs were taken by the author.

Library of Congress Cataloging-in-Publication Data.
Kingman, Henry.
   Short bike rides in and around San Francisco / by Henry Kingman — 2nd
      edition
          p.   cm. — (Short bike rides series)
   ISBN 0-7627-0214-1
   1. Cycling—California—San Francisco Metropolitan Area—Guidebooks.
   2. San Francisco Metropolitan Area (Calif.)—Guidebooks. I. Title.
   II. Series.
GV1045.5.C22S265   1998
796.6'4'0979461—dc21   98-16677
                                                             CIP

 This book is printed on recycled paper.
Manufactured in the United States of America
Second Edition/First Printing

To cyclists without cars

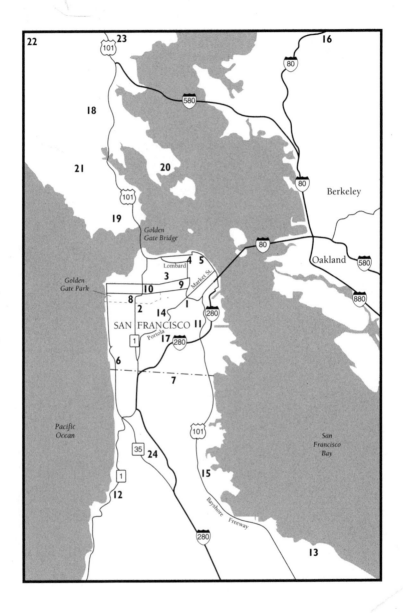

Contents

Ride Name	Recreation	Tourist	Transportation*
1 City Survey I		●	
2 City Survey II		●	
3 City Survey III		●	
4 City Survey IV		●	
5 Ring around the City Part I		●	
6 Ring around the City Part II		●	
7 Ring around the City Part IIII		●	
8 Golden Gate Park	●	●	
9 Midtown Mosey			●
10 Haight to Golden Gate			●
11 Sneaky Crosstown Route			●
12 Planet of the Apes Road	●	●	
13 Foster City Flats	●		
14 Central Peaks	●	●	
15 SFO Ramble			●
16 Port Costa Loop	●	●	
17 Two Sides of Town			●
18 Marin Freeway			●
19 Headlands Loop	●	●	
20 Paradise Loop	●		
21 Muir Woods Loop	●		
22 Alpine Dam Loop	●		
23 China Camp Agnolo	●		●
24 The Freeway South			●

* Check these rides out if you are interested in using the bicycle as your vehicle in San Francisco

Easy	Partially Rural	Challenging	Low Traffic	
		●		**1**
●				**2**
		●		**3**
		●		**4**
●			●	**5**
●			●	**6**
		●		**7**
●	●		●	**8**
●			●	**9**
●			●	**10**
		●	●	**11**
●	●		●	**12**
●	●		●	**13**
		●	●	**14**
				15
●	●		●	**16**
	●	●		**17**
				18
	●	●	●	**19**
	●	●	●	**20**
	●	●		**21**
	●	●	●	**22**
	●	●		**23**
		●		**24**

Acknowledgments

Thanks to Carolyn Helmke and Darryl Skrabak for route suggestions and editing; to Erik Jones for route suggestions; and to Patrick Morris, Laurel Segal, Brett Eilers, John Stamstad, Carolyn Helmke, Vicky Swart, Ken Eichstaedt, and especially, Greg Landtbom for being photo models.

Introduction

This book is for you if: (a) you're new in town and want to discover the most popular rides in the area; (b) you're a tourist who wants to see a different side of America's most visited city, a side you can view only from the seat of a bicycle; or (c) you're a Bay Area resident who wants to learn some extremely cool, tucked-away little bicycle routes that might otherwise take you years of exploring to discover.

You will not need a car to do any of these rides. All routes were researched and recorded using 100 percent human power. Well, that and public transportation. Most rides start right in San Francisco. Others can be accessed through connections with other rides that start in town or via public transportation. About half the routes are inside the city limits. The other half go through nearby open space and rural areas. We are truly blessed here by large areas of open space nearby where you can ride with the illusion of being miles and miles from civilization.

In his 1940 book on San Francisco, late *Chronicle* columnist Herb Caen notes, "San Francisco is a constant challenge to exploration." This is certainly true for cyclists. The San Francisco Bay Area is both hilly and full of traffic. Yet, despite the alertness and fitness required, more and more people here are making the bicycle their vehicle of choice. It's cheaper and less of a hassle than a car and faster than a bus. Cyclists can also take satisfaction in knowing that they aren't contributing to the "Gray Area's" worsening pollution and congestion.

If you're a tourist, there's no better way to get a real sense of the city than to ride a bike through it. You'll get to more places than you could on foot, yet still enjoy direct interaction with the environment and locals. Whether you're a tourist or a local, you can take pride in conquering the hills and learning to get along peaceably in traffic.

Many San Franciscans come to live here from somewhere else. If they are cyclists, the first thing most do is get lower gears. There are ways to get around climbing hills, and lots of people even ride single speeds here, but low gears will give you access to the really fun stuff, away from the traffic that tends to clog the valleys. Recreational riders should get a triple chainring crankset, or a long-arm rear derailleur and the largest cog it can accommodate. Racer types should put on a 24 cog for most out of town riding. A 26 is good for in-town cycling.

Over time, you will develop skills at dealing with both hills and city traffic. If you are new to urban cycling, please take care. If you want to go fast, get out of town or at least confine your efforts at speed to the uphill sections. It takes years, and an intimate knowledge of the city, to develop the kind of sixth sense for traffic you see demonstrated by the best bike messengers.

Motorists in San Francisco are very accustomed to and accommodating of cyclists. Traffic speeds on nearly every street are slow enough that a bicyclist can blend in easily and feel comfortable. You see cyclists riding on virtually every street in town, though some routes are definitely more popular.

Naturally, there are many different ideas about what constitutes a good bike route. Some people are extremely fearful of cars and will choose to ride on streets like Hugo, Page, or Pacific, putting up with a stop sign on every corner in order to escape car traffic. Others, faster, more experienced, or just foolhardy, will do the Oak Street Time Trial, attempting to ride from Golden Gate Park to Gough Street while hitting all the green lights. You have to average 25 mph, even over the hills, and get along in bumper-to-bumper traffic. The routes I favor travel at a pace somewhere in between. Do explore for yourself, though. As the old saw goes, your mileage may vary.

At this time bicycle traffic is still an afterthought to city planners, although the San Francisco Bicycle Coalition, with support from the growing numbers of critical mass riders, is starting to accomplish things. One of the most important changes is a new network of bicycle routes. The San Francisco Smart Yellow Pages include a map of this network.

Because the rides are complex, they may take patience and a little concentration to learn. Once you have them down, though, your perseverance will pay off the first time you get to take someone else along. If you're like me, you'll find a lot of satisfaction in sharing a good bike ride with a friend.

The maps in this book have been kept simple for easy reading.

Should you find yourself off the map while riding in the city and unsure how to get back on, look for any of the thousands of covered glass bus stops. Unless vandalized, these have street maps. If riding out of town, take an area map along.

Wherever or whenever you ride, carry extra clothing. Weather here is unpredictable and can change dramatically as you ride from microclimate to microclimate. For example, across the bridge in Marin, the temperature is usually 10 degrees warmer. But it might be foggier and colder. A summer day might start out at 80 degrees and sunny and, within a few hours, chill down to a foggy 50 degrees. Be ready. Arm- and leg-warmers are really the ticket. At least take a windbreaker.

Look out for trolley tracks and other metal surfaces when it's damp out. They become almost magically slippery when wet.

A word about air: The good kind is colder. Polluted air is warm. In traffic, breathe when you feel cool air on your face. There is usually enough air movement that after a few seconds you'll be able to get a good, fresh lungful of sea air.

If you are the kind of rider who loses his or her cool in traffic—who has angry run-ins with cars and drivers—give everybody a break and peace out. Riding safely in traffic means literally getting along with all the other road users, even those who may choose vehicles less physically, mentally, and environmentally healthy than yours.

Drivers make mistakes. Some have bad attitudes. The same holds true of bicycle riders. As the referees and police officers of the world will tell you: no harm, no foul. It's not worth getting angry about. Wave it off, suppress the adrenaline rush, and get along down the road. You have to pick your fights in life. Bad drivers just aren't worth the aggravation.

If, on the other hand, you are involved in an accident, treat it as you would a motor-vehicle collision. Don't just shake yourself off and claim that you're fine. Wait a minute or two, then take stock of things. Get the other party's name and insurance company. Call the police if the driver won't cooperate. Get the names and numbers of any witnesses.

Police statistics claim that more than half of car-bicycle accidents are the fault of the cyclist, but in many cases, such as those in which the driver opens a door into the cyclist's path, the driver is in violation of the vehicle code and potentially liable for damages. Unfortunately, many people, including some policefolk, labor under the misconception that cycling in traffic is so inherently hazardous that accidents are the logical result and cyclists are always responsible. Know your rights. Ride carefully.

But don't forget to enjoy yourself. With a little practice and constant attention to your surroundings, you will soon feel at ease and discover the satisfaction of being self-reliant and self-propelled. If you're a tourist, you'll feel privileged to see so much of San Francisco's beauty so immediately and efficiently. If you're a local, you'll soon be among the growing community of folks who get around by bicycle. In which case I'm sure I'll be seeing you—it's a pretty small town.

Whoever you are, I hope you enjoy my book. I put a lot of legwork into it, and I hope you get something out of it. If you have any suggestions or comments about these routes, especially if you have mistakes to report, please write to me in care of The Globe Pequot Press, P.O. Box 833, Old Saybrook, Connecticut 06475, or send e-mail to hkingman@best.com

City Survey Part I

Number of miles:	15
Approximate pedaling time:	1–2 hours
Terrain:	Steep hills
Traffic:	Medium
Things to see:	South of Market, skid row, museum row, Multimedia Gulch, Mission Rock Row, Potrero Hill, true crookedest street in SF, Mission district, Balmy Alley murals, Mission Dolores, Dolores Park, Noe Valley, Upper Market overpasses, The Castro/Eureka Valley

A note about the four-part City Survey rides: The first four rides, City Survey I–IV, form a cloverleaf-shaped, 49-mile-long course through San Francisco's primary tourist and commerce strips. These rides are for cyclists who want to see the people and businesses of the city. You will enjoy these rides most if you are comfortable riding in traffic and you ride at times of light traffic.

Start at Market and Fourteenth. Across Market and up the hill, note the San Francisco Mint, perched securely atop a massive natural pedestal of serpentine, the distinctive green state rock of California. The rail yard at the foot of the Mint harbors vintage trolley cars being restored for use on the Market and Embarcadero lines.

Turn right onto Fourteenth Street, which has a narrow right lane. You should be able to ride as fast as the cars and enjoy a whole lane to yourself. After about 6 blocks, make a left onto Folsom.

Folsom doesn't look like much during daylight, but this street draws big crowds on weekend nights, when it becomes the main

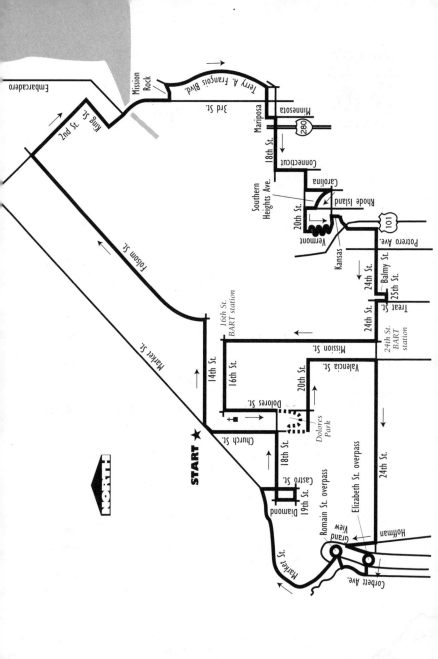

DIRECTIONS at a glance

0.0	Begin at Market/Fourteenth. Head east on Fourteenth, which is a one-way street.
0.7	Left onto Folsom Street.
2.3	Right onto Second Street.
2.8	Right onto King Street.
3.2	Left onto Third Street. Cross Lefty O'Doul drawbridge.
3.4	Left onto Mission Rock.
3.5	Right onto Terry A. François Boulevard.
4.2	Continue straight onto Mariposa.
4.4	Left onto Minnesota.
4.5	Right onto Eighteenth Street.
4.9	Left onto Connecticut.
5.1	Right onto Twentieth Street.
5.3	Left onto Carolina.
5.5	Right onto Southern Heights Avenue.
5.6	Right onto Rhode Island.
5.7	Left onto Twentieth Street.
5.9	Left onto Vermont.
6.0	Right onto sidewalk/bike path.
6.1	Bike path becomes overpass above 101.
6.2	Left onto Vermont Street.
6.5	Right onto Twenty-fourth Street.
7.0	Left onto Balmy.
7.1	Right onto Twenty-fifth Street.
7.2	Right onto Treat Street.
7.3	Left onto Twenty-fourth Street.
7.6	Right onto Mission Street.
8.5	Left onto Sixteenth Street.
8.9	Left onto Dolores Street.
9.1	Right at Eighteenth into Dolores Park.
9.6	Left onto Twentieth Street.
10.0	Right onto Valencia Street.
10.5	Right onto Twenty-fourth Street.
11.6	Right onto Hoffman.

11.8 Left onto Grand View.
12.0 Right onto overpass.
12.2 Right onto Corbett Avenue.
12.5 Right onto Romain.
12.6 Continue on overpass.
12.7 Right onto Market Street.
13.7 Right onto Castro Street.
13.9 Right onto Nineteenth Street.
14.0 Right onto Diamond.
14.1 Right onto Eighteenth Street.
14.6 Left onto Church Street to Market and Fourteenth.
15.0 End.

stem of the South of Market nightclub district. Some businesses of note on Folsom are: Big Nate's Barbecue, owned by former Golden State Warriors center and Hall of Famer Nate Thurmond; Hamburger Mary's, a lesbian-friendly bar and restaurant named for a Beulah-like character in Jack Black's prebeat classic *You Can't Win;* and The Covered Wagon, a bike messenger hangout and nightclub.

Several streets South of Market have especially pronounced character. Sixth Street is skid row, more or less, although down near Market it lays claim to perhaps the best Vietnamese restaurant in town, Tu Lan. Try #39, or the veggie spring rolls, or the chicken fried rice.

Third Street is convention and museum row, with the new SF Museum of Modern Art, designed by Mario Botta, and the Yerba Buena Center to the left off Folsom.

Turn right at Second through the so-called Multimedia Gulch, a center for electronic publishing enterprises. There's also a bike shop, Start to Finish, at the corner of Second and Brannan. When Second ends on King Street, turn right, then left onto Third Street. Cross the Lefty O'Doul drawbridge. Make the next left, onto Mission Rock, then turn right onto Terry A. François Boulevard (named for the city's first African-American supervisor) and cruise along the waterfront.

Vehicular occupancy is sometimes tolerated on François, depending on the disposition of the mayor of the day.

When François Boulevard ends, continue straight on Mariposa. Cross Third Street, a major surface artery soon to have an electric trolley line. Then make a left onto Minnesota. Many warehouses near here have been converted to residential lofts and artist studios. Make a right onto Eighteenth and begin the climb over the freeway and up Potrero Hill.

Eighteenth Street is the main commercial thoroughfare of the Hill. Look for Farley's on the left, a great coffee stop, and Bloom's on the right, which boasts the best view of any bar in town.

At Connecticut, turn left and climb for 2 blocks. At Twentieth, turn right for 3 blocks, then turn left for the steep haul up Carolina. Once up top, sing a round of "Nothing could be finer than the view from Carolina" before turning right on Southern Heights, another street with great views of downtown.

The views from atop Potrero Hill are among the finest in the city. This is also among the sunniest districts, as fog rarely reaches all the way to the Hill. Despite these advantages, this quiet district enjoyed a reputation for low rents—and high crime—for many years.

When Southern Heights ends on Rhode Island, go right briefly before turning left onto Twentieth. Take Twentieth to the end and check out the view of the Mission and of Noe and Eureka valleys. Then ride back up Twentieth a short way and turn right onto Vermont, the true crookedest street in San Francisco. Vermont's corkscrew roadway here is much tighter and maybe even a little steeper than the infamous Lombard (which we'll get to in City Survey Part IV), though Vermont lacks the flower gardens and you won't find any tourist crowds standing around with videocams—and it has only seven turns to Lombard's eight.

At the bottom of Vermont, look for a sidewalk-bike path on the right. This leads to a pedestrian-bike overpass that crosses the 101 freeway. Once across the overpass, turn left onto Vermont Street and ride past the back of San Francisco General Hospital.

There is a clause in the City Charter of San Francisco decreeing that no one shall be denied emergency health care, and it is to Gen-

eral that persons without medical insurance are usually taken. The huge autoclaves and laundry here operate in the mornings, producing an immense cloud of steam visible throughout the city.

At Twenty-fourth Street, turn right. Cross busy Potrero Avenue and continue into the lively Twenty-fourth Street Mission neighborhoods.

If you are hungry, I'd recommend stopping at one of the numerous Panaderias, Mexican bakeries with inexpensive and delicious pastry, bread, and cakes. If you're really hungry, you might want to experience a true San Francisco Mission Burrito. In my opinion, at this time, El Castillito, on Twenty-fourth and Treat, is absolutely, without question, THE SOURCE of ultimate burritodom. Get the Pollo Mojado—the Wet Chicken. Be warned, though: As my comic friend Bret puts it, "It's more than a meal. It's a two-day internal pet."

Moving right along, look out for Balmy Alley, a tiny, easy-to-miss lane just before Treat Street. Balmy boasts thirty-one Mexican murals, many quite fine. It's like getting to ride your bike in a museum. Other alleys also have murals, including Clarion, off Mission near Seventeenth Street, which features one by local filmmaker and 'zine celeb Greta Shred that is dedicated to cycling. When Balmy ends at Garfield Square, go around the block and continue heading west on Twenty-fourth Street.

When you get to Mission Street, make a right. There's a lot going on here. You may want to walk your bike along the sidewalk, the better to appreciate the ambience. Lanes are narrow on Mission, but traffic is fairly slow. If you ride it, pay attention.

At a little more than 7¼ miles, Mission is San Francisco's longest street. As a continuation of El Camino Real, it is part of a historical trade route that runs from Loretto, in Baja California, to Sonoma County, connectng many missions along the way.

At Sixteenth, turn left, ride 3 blocks, and make a left on Dolores. To your right stands the oldest remaining building in San Francisco. Completed in 1791, the Mission of Saint Francis de Assisi was named for the Doctor Dolittle of the saint world, the guy who loved animals so much he learned their languages. Everyone called it the Mission Dolores, though, after a nearby lagoon. The first Mass took place here five days prior to the signing of the Declaration of Independence in Philadelphia. Who says there's no history in the West?

A very nifty cemetery next to the Mission contains the remains of many persons remembered by history, alongside the vanished and forgotten: Arguello, first California governor under Mexican rule; Casey and Cora, outlaws hanged by the Vigilance Committee in 1856; and in the back in unmarked graves, hundreds of Costanoans, indigenous here. The painted ceiling inside the Mission is based on the chevron patterns of Costanoan basketweave and is supposed to be the single surviving artifact from their culture.

Continue on Dolores up to Dolores Park. As you ride, see if you can spot any "yardbirds." These exotic, tropical songbirds and brightly colored parrots were once domestic captives. Since escaping from their cages, they have adapted to life in the palm-studded median of Dolores.

When you see Dolores Park on the right, turn into it and ride parallel to Dolores up the path. A spectacular downtown view awaits. Continue on as the path circles right. Look for some stairs and a small bridge on the left. Take them over the trolley tracks, then make a left onto a small path. At the top corner of the park, turn left onto Twentieth and drop back down to Valencia.

Turn right from Twentieth onto Valencia. Traffic speeds are a little fast here, but Valencia is a cultural mecca, with all sorts of alternative and bohemian cafes, video stores, performance spaces, and the like. Check out Leather Tongue Video, Herban Ecology, the ATTA Gallery, and Good Vibrations. At Twenty-fourth, turn right and head up the hill into Noe Valley.

Noe Valley is a yuppie neighborhood. Not as yuppie as, say, the Marina or Cole Valley, but definitely yupped. The proximity of its tame, quiet blandness to the lively, soulful Mission is one of the great coups of juxtaposition in our city.

Continue on past the boutiques, bars, espresso bars, and restaurants with foreign names and white tablecloths. Or stop at Real Foods for a $3.00 organically grown mango. Hoist an Anchor at the Rat and Raven (Anchor Steam is brewed locally back on Potrero Hill). Whatever it takes to get you ready.

8

Ready for what, you ask? You had to ask, didn't you. PAIN is what you're getting ready for. See that hill ahead? See your bicycle? Any questions?

If you're up to it, you're in for a real treat at the top. It isn't just that the view is great. Which it is. At the top, besides dipping into the Upper Market district for a few mellow blocks, you'll learn an elegant, exclusive little bicycle route that many cyclists who've lived here for years don't know about. Come on, how can you pass that up?

Sure, you could make a right onto Castro and climb over to Eureka Valley the easy way, following the old trolley car alignment that paved the way to middle-class settlement of these parts in 1887. You could pick up the route again on Eighteenth Street. But you'd be missing out on something really cool, let me tell you. What are you anyway, human or mouse?

When you get to Hoffman, you can avoid the steepest block of Twenty-fourth by turning right onto Hoffman. Take it until it runs into Grand View, then turn left. After a short distance, you can hop up on the sidewalk and begin climbing the (gasp) Spiral Overpass!

I told you it was cool.

Continue on over Market Street and shift to your lowest gear to climb up the path to Corbett, where you make a right and ride a few blocks. The next turn is a right onto Romain. Another overpass takes you back over Market Street. This time, exit onto Market Street. Wait until all the cars have gone. The traffic light a ways up metes them out in thirty- to forty-five-second bursts. When it's clear, put yourself in a speed tuck and sail on down.

When Market begins to level and straighten out into its alignment with the top of Twin Peaks, look for Castro Street, make a right, and ride on into the Castro, the city's principal gay quarter.

In 1972 San Francisco passed an ordinance, the first of its kind, forbidding discrimination in employment or housing on the basis of sexual orientation. That, combined with San Francisco's reputation of not merely tolerating but embracing people and groups ostracized elsewhere, has made San Francisco a mecca for gays.

What other city, for example, would allow a bankrupt rice speculator to declare himself Norton, Emperor of America and Protector of Mexico? Emperor Norton would have been a bum anywhere else; here he and his two small dogs were respected and eventually regarded as municipal treasures. The Castro is San Francisco's gayest neighborhood, and you will see many bars and other businesses serving the gay community.

On the left notice the Castro Theater, a grand movie palace from the 1920s. A real live pipe organist accompanies the ushering in of patrons on certain days of the week. They play great movies at the Castro. At least a fifth of all refrigerators in town have the Castro schedule magnetically affixed to them, right next to the one for the Red Vic.

Our route continues on Castro up to Nineteenth, then loops around with a right onto Diamond and another right onto Eighteenth. Continue on Eighteenth to Church and hang a left. A few blocks later you'll come to Market Street. Fourteenth Street, where this ride began, lies a hundred yards to the right.

Haight and Fillmore, where Part II of the City Survey begins, lies a few blocks away. Cross over Market, jog left 1 block on Herman, a right onto Fillmore, up the Hill, and you're there. Are you tired yet?

City Survey Part II

Number of miles:	14.4
Approximate pedaling time:	1–2 hours
Terrain:	One climb
Traffic:	Medium
Things to see:	Lower Haight, the Haight Ashbury, Hunter S. Thompson's pad, UCSF, Sutro Forest, Laguna Honda, Inner Sunset, Outer Sunset, Ocean Beach, Outer Richmond, Inner Richmond, Laurel Heights, Divisadero Street

This ride runs out to the Pacific Ocean and back in a big loop around Golden Gate Park. It encompasses some of the quieter parts of town, yet you might be surprised at the thriving commercial strips through what most San Franciscans think of as the boondocks.

In comparison with the other three parts of the tour, this one is a little short on dramatic vistas. The neighborhoods it passes through tend to be cooler, and are more likely to be socked in with fog. The riding is a little less demanding, though by no means flat. There is one four- to ten-minute climb on a forested road near the geographic center of the city, but other than that it's mostly flat, to tell the truth. Well, flat by San Francisco standards.

Begin at the corner of Haight and Fillmore in the heart of the Lower Haight district. This area is a small mecca of great restaurants, bars, and coffeehouses. The Lower Haight feels to me like the most Bohemian of San Francisco's streets, although Valencia Street and the Mission district may have strong claim to that distinction. Spaghetti Western, favorite breakfast spot of many a pierced and tattooed young citizen, offers bicycle parking inside if it's not too crowded.

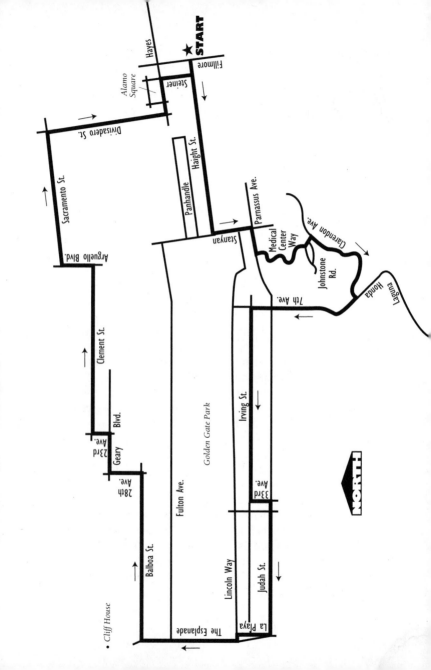

DIREC-TIONS
at a glance

0.0	Start at Haight and Fillmore. Go west on Haight.
1.3	Left onto Stanyan.
1.6	Right onto Parnassus.
1.8	Left onto Medical Center Way.
2.5	Left onto Johnstone Road.
2.7	Right onto Clarendon.
3.5	Right onto Laguna Honda/Seventh Avenue.
4.5	Left onto Irving Street.
6.1	Left onto Thirty-third Avenue.
6.3	Right onto Judah Street.
7.0	Right onto La Playa.
7.4	Left onto Lincoln Way.
7.5	Right onto The Esplanade.
8.3	Right onto Balboa.
9.7	Left onto Twenty-eighth Avenue.
9.9	Right onto Geary Boulevard.
10.3	Left onto Twenty-third Avenue.
10.4	Right onto Clement Street.
11.6	Left onto Arguello Boulevard.
11.8	Right onto Sacramento.
12.8	Right onto Divisadero.
13.8	Left onto Hayes.
14.0	Right onto Steiner.
14.2	Left onto Haight to Fillmore.
14.4	End.

The Toronado, a bar on the left, serves rad Belgian Lambic ales, along with about a hundred other kinds, mostly microbrews.

At Divisadero Street the neighborhood's commercial strip hangs a right, whereas our route continues up the hill, out of Old San Francisco and into the boondocks. At one time, before the Western Lands were annexed, Divisadero marked the city limits.

After riding past Buena Vista Park on the left, you'll enter the Haight Ashbury.

Out-of-towners always ask directions from bicyclists. Sometimes, when especially shaggy and tie-dyed ones ask directions to the Haight Ashbury—"Hey, man . . . like, know where the Haight Ashbury is, man?"—I tell 'em, "Oh man, you missed it. It was back there about thirty years ago."

Haight Street was named for Gordon Haight, who was elected governor of California in the 1880s on a platform of ending the "Yellow Peril"—immigration from Asia. If he knew that his name, thanks to Haight Street, came to stand for drugs, free love, peace, compassion, and idealism, if not civil rights, he'd probably be doing cartwheels in his coffin.

During the "Summer of Love," 1967, the city experienced a kind of paisley peril. According to police figures, 75,000 tie-dyed pilgrims arrived at Hippie Mecca on the heels of major media attention to Timothy Leary's Human Be-In (held at a site visited on the Golden Gate Park tour). The flower-child honeymoon glow is said to have lasted a whole summer before the bummer phase kicked in, along with drug addiction, poverty, jealousy, and violence. If you are interested in touring around places of hippie history, pick up Stanus Fluoride's Hippie Map, an excellent poster-type guide available at most shops on Haight Street.

At present, the flower-child legacy of the Haight Ashbury lives on in the form of homeless street kids hanging out in front of the Coffee Zone at Fillmore. Dozens and dozens of spendy boutiques sell tie-dyes and drug paraphernalia to tourists from the Midwest. Others cater to San Francitizens, selling vintage clothing imported from Midwestern thrift shops.

Almost all the old hippie havens are long gone. All You Knead, an inexpensive restaurant, is only eleven years old but has the right spirit. Robert's Hardware goes back to pre-hippie days. Park Bowl, where Jerry spaced, fell in 1997 to a giant Amoeba Records store. And of course, across the panhandle, there's the Freewheel Bike Shop, a collective you can join for an absurdly small annual fee, thereby gaining access to workstands, a solvent tank, and an excellent tool collection. Advice is free; help costs a little bit. Classes are offered. It's on Hayes near Ashbury.

Haight Street ends on Stanyan, the eastern edge of Golden Gate Park. Turn left and continue along bike shop row. There are presently seven bike shops within 4 blocks of here on Stanyan. The oldest, American Cyclery (at Frederick), dates back to 1941 and is practically a museum.

Continue up 2 steep blocks on Stanyan, then turn right onto Parnassus and begin climbing up to the University of California at San Francisco. Look on the right for number 318, where Hunter S. Thompson lived while writing his novel about the Hell's Angels, *Hell's Angels: A Strange and Terrible Saga.* His research methods apparently involved lots of late-night parties here, as well as the occasional discharging of firearms.

Another interesting building on Parnassus is number 181. It was once a farmhouse on a lonely hillside. At some point it was raised up, and two floors were built beneath it.

As the hill begins to level and you enter the campus of the University of California at San Francisco, you'll see Hillway Street on the right. Just past Hillway, look for tiny Medical Center Way on the left, turn left onto it, and begin an extended climb up through Sutro Forest.

If you don't feel up to an extended climb, continue on Parnassus down to Seventh Avenue, where you can turn right and pick up the route again.

If you just need a breather before tackling the climb, turn right from Parnassus onto the parking structure deck. Among the top medical schools in the country, UCSF enjoys a lofty perch, with views of the Golden Gate, the Park, and the Marin Headlands hills.

Medical Center Way ascends Mt. Sutro to UCSF's married-student tenements. It twists steeply through eucalyptus forest, one of many wooded legacies of mining tunnel entrepreneur, land baron, and tree planter Adolph Sutro. Many of the woodlands in the city were planted by Sutro, who didn't realize that his fast-growing import from Australia would fail as railroad tie material.

The air here is good even on high-pollution days, and for that reason it makes a great hill—repeat, hill. Keep in mind, though, that you

are on private property and that the students living in the dorms at the top need all the peace and quiet they can get. Med students aren't allowed to sleep nearly enough, you know. Don't wake them up.

When Medical Center Way ends, turn right if you want to ride all the way up to the top of Mt. Sutro, an undeveloped hill with too many trees for a nice view but with nice meadows and wooded paths. To continue on with the route, turn left onto Johnstone Drive.

To the left lies the chancellor's house, and through a small parking lot in front of it you can pick up a narrow trail leading down to the campus buildings, if you want to explore a little.

From the chancellor's house, continue on down to Clarendon and make a right. A brief climb and a long descent take you down to Laguna Honda, where you turn right and ride past Laguna Honda. Notice the concrete buttress on the sand cliff to the left. The 1989 quake left several houses up there rather askew, prompting the concrete to be poured.

When you get to Irving, make a left and ride through the heart of the Inner Sunset district.

The Inner Sunset, featuring low rents, Chinese immigrants, and lots of medical students, is kind of boring, if you ask me. The land west of Twin Peaks consisted mostly, before development, of shifting sand dunes. During earthquakes such soil liquefies, allowing unimpeded propagation of ground waves. Thus, houses in the Sunset and Richmond tend to be short and very stout. The tall, lithe, heavily festooned Victorian-Edwardian style—or "carpenter's gothic," as it was pejoratively called—had fallen from fashion by the time these districts were developed, so most of the houses here are also relatively unadorned.

Many of the houses in the Sunset were built by an architect named Doelger and were originally all painted white. The rows of white houses on the back of Twin Peaks were nicknamed the "white cliffs of Doelger."

The north–south streets in the Parkside, Sunset, and Richmond districts are numerical avenues, whereas the east–west streets between Anza and Wawona are alphabetical. It's the same system they use in Las Vegas, presumably so tourists can go around to the casinos and still be able to stumble back to the hotel later with minimal mental effort. There is little night life in the Sunset, however, although I have heard some stories about the Lost Weekend.

A high percentage of retired people live in the Sunset and Richmond. The street signs are a skosh larger, presumably for the benefit of sight-impaired drivers. Also, there are recent immigrants whose driving habits can differ surprisingly from what you might expect. Finally, despite the region's bland image, youth gangs, no doubt rebelling from the neat orderliness of it all, are said to be problematic. A lot of teenage hot-rodding goes on. An extra measure of defensiveness is called for here.

Irving is the main commerce artery of the Sunset District until about Twenty-third or so. Turn left there, past Nomad Cyclery on the left, and ride over to Judah and take a right. Judah has a great surfer coffeehouse—Java Beach—at its terminus. After a cup of Bernie's Blend, turn right onto La Playa. When that ends, go left onto Lincoln Way, cross over the Great Highway, turn right, and cruise on along the Esplanade of Ocean Beach. Put on your windbreaker! Ocean Beach is usually cold and windy.

If you want a lying-out-in-the-hot-sun-type of beach, head for Baker, 2 miles away. Take the Great Highway to Geary, turn right, then left onto Twenty-fifth Avenue and right onto Lincoln Boulevard. The north end of Baker is a nude beach. The whole beach has nice views of the Golden Gate.

To continue with this ride, climb up toward the Cliff House, a local landmark where the Ring Around the City Part II ride starts. Just before you get there, turn right onto Balboa and begin climbing up through the Outer Richmond district.

Many recent immigrants from former Soviet states and Southeast Asia live in the Richmond, as do many Jews and some older Japanese families displaced from homes in the once extensive Western Addition Japantown. Chinese also began moving here from Chinatown in the 1960s, aided by the 1964 Rumford antidiscrimination-in-housing bill.

There's a great burrito shop, Chino's Taqueria, at Thirty-fourth and Balboa. At Twenty-eighth Avenue, our route turns left. Look for a nice little view to the right at Anza. Then, at Geary, turn right.

Geary is a major automobile thoroughfare, but this far out away from town it isn't too busy. Ride a few blocks east on Geary, past the beautiful Russian Orthodox church on the left, then turn left, ride up to Clement, and turn right. Alternately, you could continue to Lake and make a right; Lake is a quiet street with a nice bike path that runs all the way to Arguello, and passes scenic Mountain Lake Park at Funston.

Ride carefully on Clement, watching out for cars backing out of the diagonal spaces. This busy street is an Asian cultural center. There are many exquisite and reasonably priced Japanese, Vietnamese, Thai, Korean, Indonesian, and Burmese restaurants and stores here. Also, look for Green Apple Books, a discount palace of titles new and used at Sixth Avenue, on the left.

When Clement ends at Arguello, go left 3 blocks and turn right on Sacramento, into upscale Laurel Heights. This neighborhood has some nice furniture shops and clothing stores, including Good Byes, a kind of thrift shop for used dress-up clothing.

At Divisadero, hang a right. Divisadero is a busy street but has some interesting storefronts, including one that houses the Church of Saint John William Coltrane, 351 Divisadero Street, near Oak. Services are offered on Sundays and include the recorded music and wisdom of JC himself, perhaps the greatest jazz saxophone player ever.

At Hayes, turn left and ride up to Alamo Square. At the top of Hayes, there's a famous postcard view of the downtown highrises in the background with a row of old Victorians turning their backs on them in the foreground.

Past Alamo Square, turn right onto Fillmore and ride 4 blocks to where this ride started, at Haight and Fillmore. Or, if you're planning to ride Part III, continue on Hayes through Hayes Valley to Octavia. Turn left there. One block later turn right onto Grove and continue to Polk, where Part III begins. Still got some life in those legs?

City Survey Part III

Number of miles:	6.9
Approximate pedaling time:	1 hour
Terrain:	A few moderate hills
Traffic:	Medium
Things to see:	City Hall, Main Public Library, Civic Center, Japantown, Pacific Heights, Harborview, Cow Hollow, The Marina, Palace of Fine Arts/Exploratorium, steepest rideable surface in San Francisco (?), Union Street, Polk Gulch

Part III starts in front of City Hall, on Grove Street at Polk. With its high green copper dome, City Hall is a replica of the U.S. Capitol building in Washington, except that our dome is 17½ feet taller. Locals delight in this fact, whereas detractors (most of whom are from Los Angeles) point to concrete evidence here of San Francisco's never underdeveloped sense of self-importance. Well, copper, anyway.

It is certainly true that San Francisco, despite its stature among the grand cities of the world, has its share of big-city problems. For years the English garden-type malls around City Hall and the buildings of the Civic Center have provided camping space for hundreds of the city's myriad homeless. The previous mayor instigated aggressive enforcement of vagrancy statutes, after which these malls stood largely empty. It really isn't much of a Civic Center, a title that, as *Ultimate San Francisco Guidebook* author Richard Delahanty points out, would be better applied to Union Square.

Also at the Civic Center: the recently built Main Public Library, Hastings College of the Law, the Civic Center BART Station, and

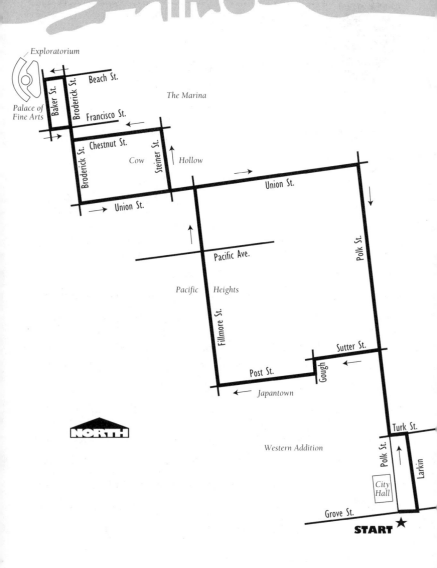

San Francisco Bay

Exploratorium

Palace of
Fine Arts

Baker St.

Broderick St.

Beach St.

The Marina

Francisco St.

Broderick St.

Chestnut St.

Cow

Steiner St.

Hollow

Union St.

Union St.

Pacific Ave.

Pacific   Heights

Fillmore St.

Union St.

Polk St.

Sutter St.

Gough

Post St.

Japantown

NORTH

Western Addition

Turk St.

Polk St.

Larkin

City
Hall

Grove St.

START ★

**DIREC-
TIONS
at a glance**

0.0	From Grove and Polk, head east on Grove.
0.1	Left onto Larkin.
0.2	Left onto Turk.
0.3	Right onto Polk.
0.6	Left onto Sutter.
0.9	Left onto Gough.

1.0 Right onto Post.
1.5 Right onto Fillmore.
2.4 Left onto Union.
2.5 Right onto Steiner.
2.8 Left onto Chestnut.
3.2 Right onto Broderick.
3.4 Left onto Beach.
3.5 Left onto Baker.
3.7 Left onto Francisco.
4.8 Right onto Broderick.
5.2 Left onto Union.
6.9 Right onto Polk to finish at Polk and Grove.

United Nations Plaza, which features an excellent farmer's market on Wednesdays and Sundays.

Head east on Grove Street; then turn left onto Larkin. Notice the new Main Public Library, completed in 1996. Inside, the giant atrium reminds me a little of the San Francisco Center shopping mall. The library has excellent indoor bike parking, but you have to buy a magnetic key for $20. At Turk make a left. Notice the lovely architecture of the Federal Building on this corner. Turn right at the next street, Polk, and continue to Sutter for a left turn. Cross Van Ness, a car driver's kind of street where traffic speeds are fast and beautiful old automobile showcases—some converted to other duties—line the street.

Everything west of Van Ness, all the way to Divisadero, was once known as the Western Addition, while beyond Divisadero lay the cemeteries and unclaimed Western Lands.

The Western Addition lost many of its old buildings to urban renewal and massive developments like the A-1, reponsible for the Geary Expressway, Saint Mary's Cathedral of the Immaculate Conception, and Japantown. This development divided the northern Western Addition in two. The north half turned into Pacific Heights, a completely gentrified neighborhood where old redwood timbered Vics were lovingly restored. The southern part is still called the Western Addition, but urban renewal took a heavy toll there.

A block past Van Ness, you'll cross Franklin, a useful, if hectic, northbound bicycling street. Continue on until, after a little bit of climbing, you can make a left onto Gough and ride toward the immense Saint Mary's Cathedral. Although from the outside St. Mary's compares unfavorably to a washing-machine turbine, it's actually kind of spectacular inside, with city views and improbable curvilinear forms to contemplate.

A right on Post Street takes you down into the commercial row of Japantown. Here, there are many great restaurants and a mall with shops full of electronic goods, pottery, paper goods, and Japanese clothing.

The present Japantown is a shadow of its former self. FBI internment programs during World War II incarcerated 112,000 Japanese-Americans—more than two-thirds of whom were American citizens—after the bombing of Pearl Harbor. Japanese from San Francisco were sent to the Topaz camp in Utah. When released, many relocated to the Richmond district.

Ride through Japantown until you get to the AMC Kabuki Theater, a large, modern movie palace with eight screens and an underground parking garage at the corner of Post and Fillmore.

South of here, Fillmore Street was once the heart of an African-American neighborhood known as the Fillmore District. This is somewhat ironic, considering President Millard Fillmore is remembered for his staunch support of the 1850 Fugitive Slave Act, an unpopular position that damaged his Whig party irreparably.

Fillmore Street was celebrated by beatnik writer Jack Kerouac for its jazz clubs and inexpensive restaurants. In the 1960s HUD urban renewal programs razed block after block of the Fillmore and then let the lots stand vacant, some for twenty years. "Urban renewal" began to sound like a euphemism for the removal of African-Americans.

At present, African-American culture thrives on Divisadero and Hayes streets, but Fillmore Street, once the heart of the district, is a bleak shell of its once lively self. If you were to turn left and ride along Fillmore south of the Geary Expressway, you'd probably agree that recent developments there hardly atone for the destruction of an entire neighborhood, hundreds of classic San Francisco buildings, and a vital cultural center, and, most tragically, for the displacement of thousands.

Turn right onto Fillmore and climb up toward the crest of the Upper Western Addition, now known as Pacific Heights. A variety of mostly expensive shops and exclusive businesses line the street and extend along California and Sacramento. Stately mansions and ritzy apartment buildings line Pacific and Broadway.

Pacific is a great crosstown street on a bicycle. There isn't much traffic up there, and the views are great. Save that for another ride, though, unless you want to make a mansion-gazing side trip. Most of the mansions are to the left; those on the right were mostly replaced with apartment houses, although the Haas-Lilienthal House Museum, down on Franklin, remains perfectly preserved. Tours are given Wednesday and Sunday afternoons for a small fee (call 415–441–3004).

Continue past Pacific to Broadway and the crest overlooking the Marina District. The road drops away dramatically. If your brakes are weak, or if you want to really appreciate the incredible view of the harbor, which stretches from the Golden Gate Bridge to the Palace of Fine Arts to Alcatraz and beyond, walk your bike down the staircase sidewalk.

Continue down to Union and make a left. Then, turn right onto Steiner and continue through Cow Hollow, named for dairy cattle once pastured here. There are a few bike shops in this area—City Cycle on Steiner and Union, Marina Cyclery on Steiner near Chestnut, and Start to Finish on Lombard at Broderick.

Cross over busy Lombard Street and make a left onto Chestnut, a small but busy commercial street in the Marina District.

The Marina was built on land reclaimed from the bay with fill. Landfill is never quite as solid as natural land, and of San Francisco's neighborhoods, this area suffered most in the Loma Prieta earthquake of 1989. Hundreds were evacuated. They camped out in the Presidio and on the Marina Green as crews worked to assess and repair the damage.

At Broderick turn right and continue down to Beach. There, turn left and ride toward the Palace of Fine Arts, built in 1915 for the Panama-Pacific International Exposition. Along with a whole row of similar buildings extending as far as Fort Mason, it was originally made of temporary materials. When it was due for destruction, local homeowner and financier Walter Johnson put up matching funds to help rebuild it with real cement. At present it houses the Exploratorium, a hands-on science museum that's fun for kids of all ages. If you stand in the center of the dome and clap your hands you get a nice echo.

Turn left onto Baker, the street in front of the Palace, and ride up to Francisco. Turn left, ride 1 block, and turn right onto Broderick. Take Broderick across Lombard and up to Union. Make a note, for future walking tours, that there are some beautiful stairs at the top of Lyon Street, 2 blocks west of here. *Also of note:* The top block of Broderick Street, a few blocks ahead, has a smooth sidewalk that may well be the steepest rideable surface in San Francisco.

Turn left onto Union, after which you'll ride a few blocks before the shopping strip begins. Then, continue on past a seemingly endless series of bars, shops, bakeries, boutiques, and movie theaters. At last, you'll cross Van Ness and climb up to Polk. There, turn right and continue through the Polk Gulch, another busy strip with more of the same: banks, cafes, galleries, people, and mendicants. Polk has a large gay contingent and is somewhat notorious, down closer to Market, for male prostitutes.

If you're done riding, continue on Polk to Grove and City Hall, where Part III began. If, on the other hand, you're feeling spry and vigorous, ready to tackle Part IV, hang a left onto California, where Part IV begins, and start heading up Nob Hill.

City Survey Part IV

Number of miles:	9.9
Approximate pedaling time:	1–2 hours
Terrain:	Steep hills
Traffic:	Intense, but slow and manageable
Things to see:	Nob Hill, Masonic Temple, Grace Cathedral, Mark Hopkins Hotel, Fairmont Hotel, Russian Hill, steepest street in San Francisco, crookedest street, Fisherman's Wharf, Hyde Street Pier, Aquatic Park, Maritime Museum, North Beach, Washington Square, Coit Tower, Filbert and Greenwich stairs, TransAmerica Pyramid, Financial District, Market Street, Union Square, Chinatown, Portsmouth Square, Polk Gulch

This part of the City Survey makes a quick run through the oldest and most visited parts of San Francisco, the number one tourist city in the world, according to the *San Francisco Chronicle.* If you have a bicycle, are comfortable riding in slow traffic, and don't mind climbing a few hills, you can see in a few hours places it takes most tourists days to get to. When you have finished this ride you'll be able to claim that you've seen most of the tourist attractions in San Francisco.

You can begin anywhere on the loop, really, but the nominal start is at the intersection of Polk and California, near where Part III of the City Survey ride ends. Head east on California, the most gradual way to climb Nob Hill. The least crowded of San Francisco's remaining

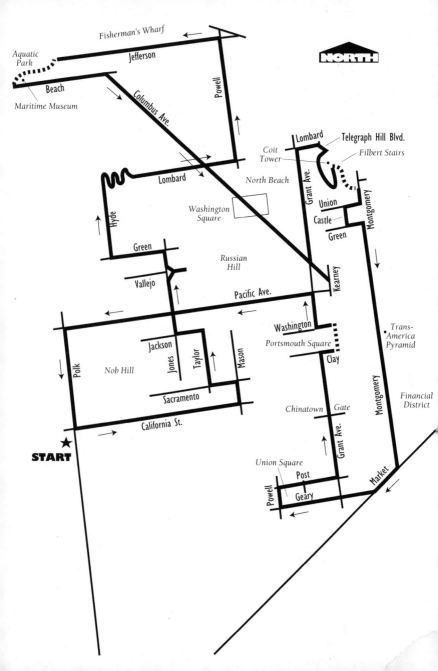

0.0   From Polk and California, head east on California.
0.6   Left onto Mason.
0.7   Left onto Sacramento.
0.8   Right onto Taylor.
1.0   Left onto Jackson.
1.1   Right onto Jones.
1.3   Right onto Vallejo.
1.4   Turn around and turn right onto Jones.
1.5   Left onto Green.
1.7   Right onto Hyde.
1.9   Right onto Lombard.
2.4   Left onto Powell.
2.7   Left onto Jefferson.
3.4   Continue on path along Aquatic Park.
3.5   Left onto path around Maritime Museum.
3.6   Left onto Beach.
3.8   Right onto Columbus.
4.9   U-turn at Kearney.
5.1   Right onto Grant Avenue.
5.4   Right onto Lombard, which becomes Telegraph Hill Boulevard.
6.0   U-turn at Coit Tower.
6.1   Pick up path on east side of Telegraph Hill Boulevard.
6.2   Left onto Filbert, down the stairs.
6.3   Right onto Montgomery.
6.4   Right onto Union.
6.5   Left onto Castle.
6.6   Left onto Green.
6.7   Right onto Montgomery.
7.5   Right onto Market.
7.6   Right onto Geary.
7.9   Right onto Powell.
8.0   Right onto Post.
8.2   Left onto Grant.
8.5   Right onto Clay.

8.6 Left into Portsmouth Square.
8.7 Left onto Washington.
8.8 Right onto Grant.
8.9 Left onto Pacific Avenue.
9.9 Left onto Polk to finish at California.

---

cable-car routes runs up California, but *be warned:* Bicycles are prohibited from hitching on, tempting though those handles may be.

In the bad old days prior to the fire and quake of 1906, Nob Hill served as pedestal for the stately mansions of the biggest tycoons in town. Charles Crocker, Leland Stanford, Mark Hopkins, and Collis P. Huntington all lived up here. They were known as the Nabobs, for some forgotten reason, or the Big Four. Nob Hill probably took it's name from Nabob. Either that, or Snob.

The Nabobs each got rich selling supplies and services to the 49ers during the gold rush. They then got together to create and control a vast real estate, railroad, and steamship company that later became Southern Pacific. You can see their red, former Southern Pacific office building down at the east end of California Street. SP was once the biggest corporation in California, and it remains the largest landowner. Nowadays, our largest corporate employer is Pacific Bell, the great information transportation company.

The great Nabob mansions are long gone, destroyed in the great quake and fire of 1906. Instead, we have the Masonic Temple, a beautifully incised art deco structure on the right, the fantastical Grace Cathedral on the left, the dignified Mark Hopkins Hotel, and the lugubrious Fairmont Hotel. And a nice view of one of the towers of the Bay Bridge down California Street.

Both the Fairmount and the Mark Hopkins have rooftop bars, and the Fairmount offers the added feature of a glass elevator. Perhaps the best free ride in the city, it's definitely worth a stop.

From California turn left onto Mason past the Fairmont, then left again onto Sacramento. Next, turn right onto Taylor, left onto Jackson, and right onto Jones to follow the contour of the slope and avoid climbing. Jones takes us over to Russian Hill.

Three blocks later on Jones, look for Vallejo, a street that splits up to the right on a small concrete ramp. Ignore the NOT A THROUGH STREET sign posted. After a short way turn right onto Vallejo Street and climb up to the top of Russian Hill, some 310 feet above the bay.

Here, you'll find a fair view of downtown and the bay over a lush but steep park. Steps lead down from here to Mason Street. Take them sometime when you don't have your bike with you. In fact, take the time to walk all around Russian Hill. There are lots of little lanes, like Marion and Macondray, and hidden gardens and lookouts.

When you've had your fill of view, ride back down to Jones and make a right. Then, make the next left, onto Green, and a right onto Hyde.

At Filbert look to the right down the supposedly steepest street in San Francisco.

A block later, Lombard, to the right, claims to be the Crookedest Street in San Francisco. Our route turns right onto Lombard and descends the chicane. (Yee-haw!)

Personally, I do not agree that Lombard is the crookedest street in town. That would be Vermont, covered in City Survey Part I, with explanation given there. As for the Tourist Bureau's claim that Filbert between Leavenworth and Hyde is our steepest street, well, that may be, but since it is one-way, it can't legally be climbed, so what good is it anyway? Furthermore, though it may be steep, it is extremely short, and so climbing it would not constitute nearly the challenge posed by, say, Elizabeth Street between Hoffman and Grandview, the top block of Stanyan, Twenty-second Street up to Vicksburg, or, heaven help you, Warren Drive. If you throw legality out of consideration, then the steepest rideable surface may very well be the sidewalk of Broderick, up to Broadway. Try that one sometime—you'll want low gears. Kearny up from Broadway is pretty brutal as well, but again, illegal to ride in that direction.

Anyway, turn right onto Lombard and proceed down the eight switchbacks of the second crookedest street in San Francisco. *Beware* of backpedaling, camera-wielding tourists, loose bricks, and idling automotive/burning brake pad effusions. See how many cars you can pass on the way down.

Continue on Lombard 4 more blocks to Powell, where you can make a left. At Jefferson an awkward left takes you into Fisherman's Wharf.

Believe it or not, Fisherman's Wharf was once so far out of town that people wouldn't go there. A guy known as Honest Harry Meiggs built the first pier. The popular, well-known Meiggs first attempted to establish a shipping pier, then, later, when that failed to attract business, an amusement area with restaurants serving clam chowder on Sunday. After years of slow business, he realized that he would soon find himself unable to meet the payments on the terms of the loans he had taken to build the place.

As the story goes, Meiggs went around to all the biggest banks in town. Such was Honest Harry's reputation that on just the power of his firm handshake he gathered about a quarter million dollars, cash. Booty in tow, Meiggs sailed down to Peru, where he went on to become a railroad baron and practically a national hero, building railroads to remote places through the steep Andes where others didn't believe they were feasible. He became the Nabob of Peru.

Eventually, word trickled up to San Francisco of Meiggs's whereabouts. Apparently, Honest Harry then lived up, at least in part, to his nickname, sending large sums to his San Francisco creditors. The governor pardoned him. He became more admired here than ever. He was even sent an invitation to return and speak to the public but, perhaps fearful of retribution, never quite made it back.

Looking at Fisherman's Wharf today, it is difficult to imagine it was ever a financial liability. Especially in summer, tourists pack the outdoor seafood stalls, shops, galleries, and bars. Street performers can make hundreds of dollars a day, a quarter at a time. Tourists line up to board ferry boats bound for Alcatraz and other points around the bay. They rent bicycles or hire pedal-powered lorries to ride around in. Money flows like a runaway train. Pier 39, to the right along the Embarcadero, ranks with Disneyland and Disney World in annual visitorship figures.

When Jefferson ends in Aquatic Park, continue on the path along the bay for a few hundred yards, past the bleachers, and turn left onto

the path that wraps around the far side of the Maritime Museum, a boatlike art deco structure built by the Works Project Administration during the Depression as a bathhouse. Or, if you have time, you might want to continue on the path to Ghirardelli Square, an old chocolate factory converted to boutique duty. Check it out, return, and ride up to Beach Street.

After riding up to Beach, turn left. At the corner of Beach and Hyde, note the Buena Vista Cafe on the right, where Irish coffee was invented.

A few blocks farther, look for a slanting right onto Columbus. Note Joseph Conrad park, a tiny island in this intersection, named for a virtually uneducated sailor who became one of the great literary voices the world has ever heard. Sometime, read *Lord Jim*.

Continue on Columbus into North Beach.

Originally an Italian ghetto, North Beach served as the Bohemian quarter during the Beat era written about in Kerouac's *Dharma Bums* and other works. The beats crowed so loudly about the good weather, great food, and low rents of North Beach that fame overtook it. Today, it remains too fashionable to be cheap, but maintains some boho ambience and plenty of great restaurants and bars.

The word *beatnik*, incidentally, was coined by Herb Caen, who decided that the so-called beat poets had so much in common with the Russian space probe Sputnik—both were "far out"—that their names should be merged. Of all Caen's myriad compounds and amalgamations, *beatnik* is said to be his legacy, his biggest contribution to the common parlance.

At 841 Columbus, you can visit Lyle Tuttle's Tattoo Museum, from noon to 8:00 or 9:00 P.M. (415–775–4991).

Soon, you'll pass Washington Square. There is a statue here of Ben Franklin, which is featured on the cover of great San Francisco author/poet Richard Brautigan's *Trout Fishing in America*. Behind it thrust the twin spires of Saints Peter and Paul Roman Catholic Church, where Joe DiMaggio married Marilyn Monroe. Actually, some people claim that the two had to be wed elsewhere because both had been previously divorced and that they came here afterward for the famous publicity photos. On the right note the Washington

Square Bar and Grill, the oft-plugged watering hole of San Francisco's more sodden journalists.

When you get to Broadway, you'll see the Condor Club on the left, where Carol Doda took off her top during the Republican National Convention in 1964, becoming the first topless dancer in America. The Supreme Court ruled that nudity in and of itself was not pornographic, and in 1969 Doda became the first bottomless dancer. Nowadays, she runs a lingerie store on Union in the Marina.

Former 49er-great Joe Montana, considered by most San Franciscans to be the greatest quarterback since John Brodie, if not ever, bought the Condor in the early 1990s, removed the landmark neon sign of Doda, and turned it back into a regular bar. Lots of other bars near here carry on the topless tradition, though.

Actually, the bawdy tradition goes back further on Pacific Street, 1 block south of Broadway. Terrific Pacific, as the sailors called it, was once the heart of a district so vice-ridden it was known as the Barbary Coast.

After crossing Broadway you'll see City Lights Bookstore, owned by great San Francisco beat poet and painter Lawrence Ferlinghetti. Ferlinghetti opened City Lights in 1953 as America's first all-paperback bookstore. He also began publishing magazines and books with help from the local beat talent. Allen Ginsberg's *Howl* was the title that really put City Lights on the map. Obligatory tourist activity: Pick up a copy of *Howl* at City Lights and have them stamp the title page. Or, since you like guidebooks, try Don Herron's excellent *Literary World of San Francisco.*

This area is a region of great bars. Across Kerouac Alley from City Lights there's the ornate Vesuvio's, and across the street are the reclusive Spec's, a former speakeasy, and the dim Savoy. A block away, on Kearny, is the Albatross Brew Pub, the original microbrewery. Not to mention the House of Nan King, the inexpensive but crowded source of many amazing flavors. But I forget. We're cyclists here, health conscious and teetotaling, no doubt. Vegetarians. Better make a U-turn on Columbus and cross back over Broadway.

A hundred yards later, veer right onto Grant Avenue, a narrow row of classic old San Francisco places. There's the Lost and Found

Saloon, seemingly little changed from the days when unsuspecting sailors were shanghaied, that is, slipped Mickey Finns (a sleep-inducing concoction named for the King of the Shanghai Barmen), and shipped out unawares in the night to serve as crew on long, arduous voyages to places such as Shanghai. Some wharf bars even had trapdoors in the floor to drop the snoozing sailors through, directly into rowboats for easy transportation to awaiting ships.

Then there's the Sodini's Green Valley Basque Restaurant on Green at Grant, operating since 1908. Cafe Trieste. North Beach Pizza. The Postcard shop with the antique shooting game in front. A fun place, Grant Avenue.

Grant Avenue has many identities. Writers began noting in the 1930s that you could walk along Grant and pass through four different neighborhoods: Starting on Market you go through the Financial District, then Chinatown, North Beach, and finally the Italian ghetto of Telegraph Hill, once a humble, working-class neighborhood.

Continue up Grant into this "working-class" neighborhood. Look for a right onto Lombard and then continue straight onto Telegraph Hill Boulevard, which wends skyward up to Coit Tower. (Or, if you'd like a side trip, continue on Grant Avenue to Jack Early Park, named for the citizen who created it. The late Mr. Early passed on in January 1998.)

This phallic tower was erected with money left to the city by the notorious Lily Hitchcock-Coit. Coit enjoyed a scandalous life-style, smoking cigars, dressing like a man, and playing poker with firemen. She sympathized with the South in the Civil War and went to live in Paris when the North won. She later returned to San Francisco and when she died left $100,000 to be spent in a way that would beautify the city. Hence, Coit Tower. The designers protest allegations it was modeled after a firehose nozzle.

Inside there are beautiful murals painted by WPA artists in the 1930s. They record the contributions of the largely unsung working and laboring classes, many of whom were recent immigrants. Together with similar frescoes in the Rincon Annex Post Office and Willis Polk's Beach Chalet, which show the public at play and recreation, these murals offer a glimpse of what life was like back then.

There are fantastic views from atop Coit Tower. There are also nice views from Pioneer Park, in which it is set. The statue of Columbus in front of the tower presents a phallic protuberance of its own, if you stand in just the right place on the circular retaining wall (*Hint:* next to the parking sign on the west side).

Look for a path on the bay side of the tower's parking lot and take it downhill parallel to the road. Soon you'll see a sign marked FILBERT. Go left here and proceed down the Filbert Stairs to Montgomery. To the left is Julius' Castle, an exclusive restaurant with an amazing view. To the right is a nice little bar and restaurant called the Shadows. Across Montgomery looms the beautiful art deco Malloch Apartment Building, which you may remember seeing in Bogart and Bacall's *Dark Passage*. Straight ahead, the stairs continue, but our route turns right onto Montgomery. If you have the time and a lock with you, you may want to walk all the way down the Filbert Stairs, turn left onto Sansome, and return up the Greenwich Stairs. It's guaranteed to be a memorable experience for devotees of fine gardens and bird–watchers.

Soon, Montgomery ends and you have to go right onto Union. Look for a small alley—Castle—and take it left. Then make a left onto Green and a right back onto Montgomery.

Montgomery drops down into the Financial District, which begins after you pass the TransAmerica Pyramid, flagship of the San Francisco skyline. This sky-piercer was intended to impart a unifying identity to a company with its irons in a lot of business fires. The pointy part on top is referred to locally as the dunce cap; everything above the elevator-house shoulders is purely decorative. The windows have to pivot around and be washed from the inside—traditional window-washing scaffolds don't work on a slope. The twenty-seventh floor used to have a free viewing room, but it was closed after the Oklahoma City bombing.

Continue on Montgomery into the glass and steel canyons in the heart of the Financial District. You'll probably see a few bike messengers here, plying a difficult trade.

In San Francisco's earliest days, Montgomery was the main shopping thoroughfare. The west was the "dollar" side and the east was the "two-bit" side. It was lined with wooden sidewalks, and in the summer the trade winds filled the air with sand and splinters. The stock exchange was there, and, on the site of the present TransAmerica Pyramid, the Montgomery Block, or "Monkey Block," the first earthquake-proof building, which was built on an immense buried raft of redwood. The Monkey Block housed the Exchange bar and offered inexpensive space to many artists and writers.

The characters of the day might be encountered on Montgomery. Joshua Norton, self-declared Emperor of America and Protector of Mexico, a bankrupt rice speculator, strolled here in imperial regalia with his dogs Bummer and Lazarus. He might be delivering a proclamation to the local papers decreeing that a bridge be built across the bay to Oakland, or out to the Farallon Islands. Or he might be applying for $10 million loans that would be approved but paid for with $10.00. Or, perhaps he'd be en route to an opera or merely out to tip his hat to his many admirers.

Mark Twain, with his bushy red hair and moustache, might be found holding court in front of the cigar stand, spinning one of his trademark tall tales, or on his way to work at the local newspaper.

When Montgomery ends on Market Street, turn right onto the main commercial artery of present-day San Francisco. On a clear day, you can see Twin Peaks in the distance at one end of Market and the clock tower of the Ferry Building at the other. On either side are huge and mostly beautiful old buildings, including the Palace Hotel, built by Ralston in 1875 and rebuilt in 1909.

Some commuting cyclists favor Market Street because traffic speeds are fairly slow; however, there are many buses and taxis, and more than a few cyclists have lost their lives on Market. Many San Franciscans hope that Market will soon be closed to all traffic except buses, taxis, and bicycles.

At Geary make a right and ride 3 blocks to Union Square, which took its name from union protests in the 1860s. At present the district is a fancy shopping area swarming with tourists, but there are still occasional protests and marches here. All around are famous department stores like Gumps, Saks Fifth Avenue, Macy's, and Neiman-Marcus. The Christmas season brings on an informal window-dressing competition judged independently by thousands of strolling San Franciscans, who often meet at the tiny carnival atop the Emporium on Market.

At Powell turn right, then right again onto Post to circle around the square. Two blocks later, turn left onto Grant and continue up toward Chinatown.

If you are a Dashiell Hammett fan, you may want to make a side trip a block west at Bush. Bush is one-way, so walk your bike up the sidewalk. Soon, beneath the street sign for Burritt Alley, you'll see a plaque that says ON APPROXIMATELY THIS SPOT MILES ARCHER, PARTNER OF SAM SPADE, WAS DONE IN BY BRIGID O'SHAUGHNESSY. The reference, of course, is to the first of a series of never adequately explained murders in Hammett's classic, *The Maltese Falcon.*

At Bush you'll pass through the Chinatown Gate and enter the main tourist row of Chinatown. The sheer humanity is overwhelming. Chinatown puts on a flashy face for the tourists, but look up a few stories above the brightly painted shops and you'll see broken windows not likely to be replaced anytime soon. Overcrowding and poverty in Chinatown make it one of the poorest neighborhoods in town, despite the thriving tourist trade.

Actually, local trade thrives, too. Stockton Street, 1 block uphill, is the main commercial row for the locals and is as interesting to explore as Grant Avenue.

If you have time, ride down some of the alleys and lanes around Chinatown. Check out the laundry hanging out to dry everywhere. If you're feeling tired, buy some ginseng. Or some chop suey. Or perhaps a handmade, x-rated fortune cookie from The Golden Gate Fortune Cookie Co., at 56 Ross Alley, off Jackson between Stockton and Grant.

At Clay turn right and ride down to Portsmouth Square. When you get there, turn left into the Square and walk your bike across to the other side.

Portsmouth Square was the city center when San Francisco was but a metallic gleam in the unmined soils and rivers of Northern California and Nevada. English trader William A. Richardson founded Yerba Buena Cove here, erecting a semipermanent tent at what today would be 827 Grant Avenue. It was San Francisco's first structure, erected June 25, 1835. Four years later, the streets that today make up Chinatown were laid out. No wonder they're so narrow. At that time, prior to large bay-filling projects, the shoreline came right up to the square. In 1846 John Montgomery of the USS *Portsmouth* landed here and claimed the settlement for the United States. Of course, intermittent settlement had occurred around Mission Dolores (see City Survey Part I) since 1776.

In the square look for the Robert Louis Stevenson Monument, a pedestal with a large bronze galleon and some pithy Stevensonian wisdom.

On the other side turn left onto Washington, and then make a right back onto Grant. Take Grant to Pacific and turn left. Continue up Pacific to Polk, turn left, and ride through Polk Gulch back to California, where the ride began.

There you have it, a brief glimpse into some of the most famous places in town.

If you want to connect up with Part I and keep riding, continue on Polk to Market. Cross over Market and continue on Tenth Street. When you get to Folsom, turn left and pick up the route described in Part I.

If you have just completed the whole four-part series, congratulations are in order. Kind of a sensory overload, wasn't it? You'll sleep well tonight. And you will have seen a lot more of the town than you would have had you just taken the 49-mile drive.

Ring around the City Part I

Number of miles:	16.6
Approximate pedaling time:	2 hours
Terrain:	Flat
Traffic:	Mostly light
Things to see:	Ferry Building, Embarcadero, Pier 39, sea lions, Fisherman's Wharf, Maritime Museum, Aquatic Park, Fort Mason, Marina Safeway, Marina Green, St. Francis Yacht Club, Wave Organ, Golden Gate Promenade Rock Sculpture Garden, Fort Point, Golden Gate Bridge, Baker Beach, China Beach, Land's End, Legion of Honor, Sutro Baths, Sutro Park, Cliff House

"You can learn more by going around something than by going through." So claims the Perimeter Cycling Association, a club in Tucson, Arizona, that sponsors perimeter rides and races such as El Tour de Tucson and the Cochise Classic. Whether you agree with that philosophy or not, you probably will agree that this ride encompasses many places of great interest and beauty.

The first part passes lots of famous San Francisco tourist spots. The complete tour, including all three parts, is 42 miles long. That may not seem far, but there is a lot to see, so give yourself plenty of time. Budget a minimum of six hours for the complete tour, more if you plan on taking a few breathers at scenic spots.

The third part contains most of the climbing. As luck would have it, however, the second part of the ride ends at the Daly City BART station. Thus, if you don't enjoy hill climbing, or if you run short on

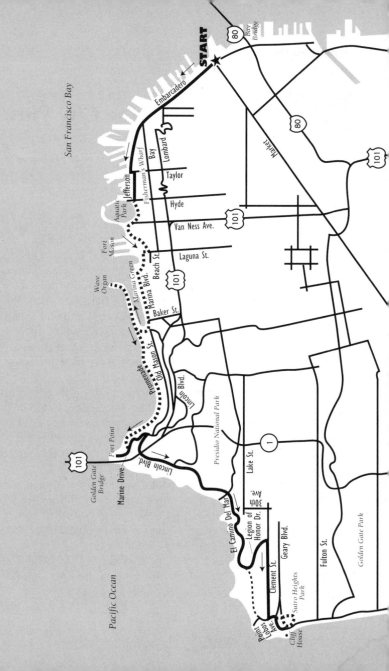

START

San Francisco Bay

Pacific Ocean

Bay Bridge

80

80

101

Market

Embarcadero

Bay

Lombard

Taylor

Fisherman's Wharf

Jefferson

Hyde

Aquatic Park

Van Ness Ave.

101

Fort Mason

Laguna St.

Beach St.

101

Marina Green

Wave Organ

Marina Blvd.

Baker St.

Promenade

Old Mason St.

Lincoln Blvd.

Fort Point

Presidio National Park

1

Golden Gate Bridge

Marine Drive

Lincoln Blvd.

Lake St.

101

El Camino Del Mar

Legion of Honor Dr.

30th Ave.

Geary Blvd.

Clement St.

Point Lobos Ave.

Cliff House

Sutro Heights Park

Fulton St.

Golden Gate Park

DIREC-TIONS at a glance

0.0	Start at Ferry Building, Market and Embarcadero.
1.9	Turn left onto Taylor.
2.0	Turn right onto Jefferson.
2.2	Jefferson ends at Hyde Street; go straight on path into Aquatic Park.
2.4	Path ends; turn right onto Van Ness Avenue; then make an immediate left past some anticar posts and up a steep hill into Fort Mason.
2.6	Stay right on red bicycle path.
2.7	At bottom of hill, go through anticar posts and turn right onto the sidewalk of Laguna Street. Ride for a few yards before turning left onto sidewalk of Beach Street.
2.8	Pick up Marina Boulevard bike path after Buchanan Street.
3.1	Path curves left; Marina Green is on right.
4.2	Turn right onto path at Baker Street.
4.3	Turn right onto Yacht Road.
4.5	Turn around at Wave Organ.
9.3	Pick up San Francisco Bay Trail/Golden Gate Promenade along waterfront.
11.3	Turn right onto Marine Drive.
11.5	Turn around at Fort Point.
12.1	Marine Drive changes name to Long Avenue. Go right onto Lincoln Boulevard.
12.3	Golden Gate Bridge Plaza on right.
13.9	Lincoln Boulevard becomes El Camino Del Mar.
15.0	Turn left onto Legion of Honor Drive.
15.4	Turn right onto Clement Street.
16.2	Turn left onto El Camino Del Mar.
16.3	Enter Sutro Heights Park.
16.5	Circle park; then turn left onto Point Lobos Avenue.
16.6	End at Cliff House.

time, you can ride the first two parts and take BART back to the Embarcadero station, a few blocks from where Part I starts. This option can cut the ride time down to, oh, say, four leisurely hours, not including BART time. Just *be aware* that bicycles are not allowed on BART during weekday commute hours.

Start at the Ferry Building on the Embarcadero at the foot of Market Street. Before the TransAmerica Pyramid was built, the Ferry Building's stately clock tower was considered the signature of the San Francisco skyline. The ferry terminal saw much more traffic before the bridges were completed in the late 1940s, but regular commuter ferry service still runs from here to Oakland, Sausalito, Tiburon, and Vallejo. Head north along the Embarcadero.

If you need to make a pit stop first, check out the Hyatt on the north side of Market just across Justin Herman Plaza. It has an immense atrium, and if you take the interior glass elevators all the way to the top floor, you'll find a rest room.

Soon you'll pass Pier One, recently fixed up nicely with new planking and benches. A little farther, Pier Seven, the fishing pier, also accommodates sightseers. Note that piers north of the Ferry Building have odd numbers, whereas those to the south have even.

Much of the present shoreline was made from landfill during the nineteenth century. Latter-day Argonauts—those who sailed around the Horn to seek their fortune in the Gold Rush of '49—abandoned thousands of ships in the bay, and many of these were plowed right under the polder when the shoreline was extended out into the bay. Fill was taken from a rock quarry on Telegraph Hill, leaving high stone cliffs visible to the left.

The shipping industry was once vital in San Francisco. After all, San Francisco Bay is one of the great natural harbors of the world. Today, Oakland, with its superior rail and trucking access, wins nearly all the shipping contracts. The newsprint pier, number 27, is the only shipping pier still in active use in San Francisco.

A luxury-liner dock north of there sees good trade, however, as does wildly popular Pier 39. According to the *San Francisco Chronicle*, Pier 39 is the third highest visited tourist attraction in the United States, ranking behind only Disneyland and Disney World, and that was before the new Underwater World attraction (415–623–5300) opened in 1996. A sidewalk leads around the pier but is often too crowded to even walk a bicycle on. The Eagle Cafe, atop Pier 39, is a famous old longshoreman and beat poet haunt that was picked up and set on top of Pier 39 to make room for a parking structure.

On the north side of Pier 39, sea lions bask and bark on floating jetties. They used to occupy the misnamed Seal Rocks just offshore from the Cliff House, where this ride ends, until the earthquake of 1989 closed Pier 45 and the sea lions moved to Pier 39.

Continuing past Pier 39, Fisherman's Wharf starts. In summer the streets will be crowded with tourists. Tons of T-shirt shops and seafood vendors ply their wares, alongside the wax museum and Ripley's Believe It or Not. There are also many art galleries here. Just past the big restaurants—Tarrantino's, Alioto's, and Fisherman's Grotto—a small marina contains fishing boats that still go out in the morning to fish for crabs and clams. Some boats are available for chartered fishing parties.

At the bottom of Hyde Street, the Maritime Museum features a variety of antique vessels. The regal *Balclutha* is typical of the Argonaut boats that sailed around the Horn prior to the installation of the Panama Canal. It made seventeen trips around Cape Horn and could sail 300 miles per day. The *Eureka* paddle-wheel ferry ran between the city and Sausalito before the Golden Gate bridge was built. It could carry 120 cars and 2,000 passengers, making the trip in twenty-seven minutes.

Hyde Street also features a popular cable-car route, the steepest in the city. And if you look up Hyde Street you'll see the Buena Vista Cafe, where Irish coffee was invented, on the corner of Beach and Hyde.

Past Hyde Street, continue on a bike path past car barricades into Aquatic Park. Members of the Polar Bear club swim in the cold bay waters here. On the left notice the boatlike building that houses the National Maritime Museum. Originally built as a casino/bathhouse by the Depression-era Works Project Administration, it never attracted the 5,000 daily bathers it was built to accommodate, and it became a museum in the 1950s.

Continue riding around the Park until you exit onto Van Ness Avenue. Go right, then left up a steep hill along the water's edge. As you climb, you'll be rewarded with postcard views of Golden Gate Bridge and Fort Mason. One and a half million soldiers passed through Fort Mason in World War II, en route to duty in the Pacific Theater. Presently, Fort Mason houses many small offices and shops, including the Mexican Museum (415–441–0404), the Museo Italo-Americano (415–673–2200), the African-American Historical and Cultural Society Museum (415–441–0640), and the SF Craft and Folk Art Museum (415–775–0990). Here you'll also find Greens, an expensive Buddhist monk–run vegetarian restaurant with a sunset view of the Golden Gate Bridge (415–771–6222), and the Magic Theater.

After scoping out the view, continue on a red bike path through the green lawn of Fort Mason. Stay right on the path as it drops down to Laguna Street. You'll see the Marina Safeway, which has a produce section notorious for its singles scene on Wednesday nights. Go right briefly on the sidewalk of Laguna, then left on the sidewalk of Beach for 1 block before picking up a red bike path along Marina Boulevard.

The path runs past the Marina Green, site of San Francisco's first airstrip. Today, kite flyers carry on the aeronautical tradition. After passing an extensive yacht harbor, note the Palace of Fine Arts to the left. Originally constructed of temporary materials for the Panama-Pacific International Exposition of 1915, the palace was simplified and reconstructed of reinforced concrete in the 1960s and 1970s. Now, it houses the Exploratorium, a hands-on science museum.

Turn right onto Pedestrian Way, just past Baker Street. When Pedestrian ends, turn right, continue through the parking lot of the St. Francis Yacht Club, and pick up the path out to the Wave Organ, where the gurgling sounds of the bay are piped up for your listening pleasure.

Retrace your route back past the Yacht Club. Stay as close as possible to the water and you'll soon pick up a multiuse path called the Golden Gate Promenade. It is unpaved in parts but plenty smooth for slow riding. Take the Promenade all the way to Fort Point, just underneath the Golden Gate Bridge.

Fort Point was built between 1853 and 1861 but became obsolete within a year of completion: Artillery was developed during the Civil War that could destroy brick forts. Nevertheless, Golden Gate Bridge builder Joseph Strauss designed the approach to straddle the fort and preserve it for its historic importance.

Climb up from the fort on Long Avenue and make a right onto Lincoln Boulevard. Lincoln climbs up to the Golden Gate Bridge Plaza, where you will find rest rooms, a snack shop, and lots of tourists. It then passes under the 101 freeway and continues climbing south past Fort Winifield Scott.

After the bridge Lincoln descends past Baker Beach, crosses a drainage, becomes El Camino Del Mar, and starts back uphill through the wildly opulent Seacliff district. Robin Williams, himself a devoted cyclist, lives here, near a giant sinkhole that swallowed an immense Tudor mansion in 1996.

Continue climbing as the road opens up into parkland. At the top, you'll see the Palace of the Legion of Honor, which houses an art museum. You may choose to continue on Camino Del Mar, which turns to passable dirt past the Legion, or you can turn left onto Legion of Honor Drive, which takes you downhill past a golf course to Clement Street. Turn right onto Clement and take it until it turns into Seal Rock and meets back with El Camino Del Mar.

Turn left onto El Camino. When it meets Point Lobos Avenue, cross over this street and pick up the entrance path to Sutro Heights Park. Follow this path around a circular promontory with commanding views of the Cliff House, Seal Rock, and Ocean Beach. If the day is clear, try to spot the Farallons, seven rocky islands 32 miles offshore that comprise the breeding grounds of many species of migratory birds.

Return to Point Lobos Avenue and descend to the Cliff House. If you wish to return to the ride start via a different route, take the Great Highway past the Cliff House down to Golden Gate Park. Follow the Golden Gate Park route (Route 8) to the Panhandle and pick up the Midtown Mosey route, which will take you to Market Street near the Embarcadero. Otherwise, turn to Part II of the loop and ride on.

Ring around the City
Part II

Number of miles:	9.3
Approximate pedaling time:	1 hour
Terrain:	Flat
Traffic:	Mostly light except for Lake Merced and Third Street
Things to see:	Cliff House, Ocean Beach, Lake Merced, Olympic Club Golf Course, Broderick/Terry duel site, San Francisco State University

This ride starts at the Cliff House and ends at the Daly City BART station. There are a few sections where traffic is heavy or shoulders less than ideal, and it passes briefly through the economically depressed area of Ingleside, but Ocean Beach and Lake Merced offer beautiful scenery, good air, and generally nice riding. This route also includes what I believe to be the best route between Lake Merced and south-central San Francisco.

Begin at the Cliff House. The original Cliff House was a grandiose seven-story castle erected by mining tunnel entrepreneur, land baron, and great tree-planter Adolph Sutro in 1858. At that time, San Francisco was a booming town on the other side of the peninsula. A trip to the Cliff House was an expedition to the country, best undertaken behind a pair of horses on Point Lobos Road. McGinn buses also left the Plaza hourly.

The first Cliff House perched on its rock mooring in a fantastic, larger-than-life way before burning down in 1907. Three succeeding Cliff Houses also burned. The present edition is a bit downscale from the original, but still offers fantastic ocean views and tasty seafood

START

★
Cliff House

Pt. Lobos Ave.

Geary Blvd.

Sutro Heights Park

Richmond District

Fulton St.

Golden Gate Park

Lincoln Way

Great Highway

multiuse path

Sunset District

NORTH

Pacific Ocean

1

Stern Grove

San Francisco Zoo

Clearfield Dr.

Sloat Blvd.

Nineteenth Ave.

Junipero Serra Blvd.

Lake

Merced

Harding Park Municipal Golf Course

Skyline Blvd.

Fort Funston

Pacific Rod & Gun Club

John Muir Dr.

Font St.

Holloway Ave.

Brotherhood Way

Beverly St.

19th Ave.

Randolph St.

Orizaba Ave.

Sagamore St.

Alemany

Lake Merced Blvd.

Daly City BART

DeLong St.

Crystal St.

Goethe St.

To Part III

280

Mission St.

John Daly Blvd.

Crocker Ave.

Guadalupe Canyon Pkwy.

82

Radio Tower Rd.

Mt. San Bruno

DIREC-TIONS at a glance

0.0	Start at Cliff House. Head south on Great Highway.
3.8	Turn right onto Skyline Boulevard.
4.3	Turn left onto John Muir Drive.
5.5	Turn left onto Lake Merced Boulevard.
6.5	Turn right onto Font Street.

6.9   Turn left onto Holloway Avenue.

7.5   Turn right onto Beverly Street.

7.8   Turn left onto Nineteenth Avenue.

8.0   Turn left onto Randolph Street.

8.4   Turn right onto Orizaba Avenue.

8.6   Cross Sagamore Street and Brotherhood Way and turn left onto Alemany Boulevard.

8.7   Go through underpass.

8.9   Turn right onto Crystal Street.

9.0   Turn right onto DeLong Street or, to continue with Part III, turn left onto Goethe Street.

9.3   End at Daly City BART.

and cocktails. Although almost a cliché, Sunday brunch oysters on the half-shell at the Cliff House are still a wonderful treat.

Just north of the Cliff House may be seen the ruined foundations of the Sutro Baths, an immense indoor bathing facility built in 1896 by Adolph Sutro. The baths burned down in 1966, and the foundations and grounds are now a crumbling urban wasteland vaguely reminiscent of pueblo cliff dwellings.

Just offshore notice the misnamed Seal Rocks, where stellar sea lions, led by the immense Ben Butler and his progeny, used to bask and bark. Then the 1989 earthquake prompted the sea lions to pick up and move to some abandoned floating piers near Pier 39, to the delight of the myriad tourists there.

Also of interest at the Cliff House is the Musée Mécanique, full of restored antique coin-op amusements and passport photo machines.

The Musée is on the bottom level, near the Camera Obscura, a dark room into which a rotating periscope projects an image of the waves, beach, and rocks.

Head downhill on the Great Highway toward Ocean Beach. On the left note Golden Gate Park extending its finger of greenery into the city. The park is ½ mile wide and 3½ miles long. The two wooden windmills at either corner of its western edge once pumped all the irrigation water that transformed the park from shifting sand dunes to green haven.

Just south of the park, a multiuse path parallel to Ocean Beach begins. The path is generally crowded with skaters and walkers, so I recommend staying on the Great Highway, which has a nice wide shoulder. Watch out for sand drifting into the shoulder, however, which can force you out into traffic. If you do want to take the path, turn left onto Lincoln Way and make an immediate right onto the path.

At 3 miles, pass Sloat Boulevard. If you wish to bypass the ride around Lake Merced you can go left onto Sloat, take it ⁷/₁₀ mile to Clearfield Drive, go right, and at the dead end go left onto Lake Merced Boulevard. After ⁵/₁₀ mile make a left onto Font and rejoin the main route.

If you do want to ride around Lake Merced (sure you do!), continue on the Great Highway up a short hill. Just beyond the crest make a right onto Skyline Boulevard. A half mile farther, take the left lane and turn left onto John Muir Drive.

After passing some apartments you will see a feature of Ring around the City Part III—Mt. San Bruno, with its many radio towers—straight ahead. To the left you may hear shots being fired at the Pacific Rod and Gun Club, a shooting range open to the public. On the right you can catch glimpses through the trees of the Olympic Golf and Country Club, one of the world's most expensive and exclusive. Only a few years ago, a discrimination lawsuit forced the Olympic Club to open its membership to women.

When Muir ends at Lake Merced Boulevard, turn left. Just after this turn you'll see a stone monument on the right with a historic marker commemorating the duel waged near here in 1859 between

U.S. Senator Broderick and California Supreme Court Chief Justice Terry. Terry was pro-slavery, and publicly maligned Broderick for being against it. Broderick missed his shot and was mortally wounded by Terry, who then sank into alcoholism and himself died a short time later. Thereafter, dueling—which had been a common and accepted method of conflict resolution in San Francisco—fell out of fashion.

Lake Merced can be a busy street during weekday rush hours, when the jogging path on the left side may be preferable. Shortly after you pass Brotherhood Way (⁴⁄₁₀ mile), a bike path begins on the right.

After passing a residential district for San Francisco State students, make a right onto Font Street and head into the campus. When you come to a roundabout, make a right and, halfway around, another right back onto Font. Go around another roundabout the same way, and then at the third roundabout, ride 270 degrees around to make a right onto Holloway Avenue. Take Holloway across busy Nineteenth Avenue, across Junipero Serra, and past a stone gatepost proclaiming TERRACES. Then make the first right onto Beverly Street.

After 3 blocks bend left onto Nineteenth Avenue, which is relatively quiet, having lost most of its volume to Junipero Serra Boulevard. There are railroad tracks to watch out for, though, which can be especially slippery if it's raining or foggy. Stay with the tracks when, 2 short blocks later, Nineteenth Avenue bends left into Randolph Street.

Randolph can be a little bit lively; keep your wits about you here if you have an affluent appearance as there are sometimes desperate-looking characters milling around. When Randolph ends, turn right onto Orizaba Avenue.

Before describing the next several turns, I'd like to offer a quote from Burton Watson's translation of Taoist philosopher Chuang Tzu. In a chapter entitled "The Secret of Caring for Life," from *Chuang Tzu Basic Writings* (Columbia University Press), a great Butcher named Ting describes his methods:

Whenever I come to a complicated place, I size up the difficulties, tell myself to watch out and be careful, keep my eyes on what I'm doing, work very slowly, and move the knife with the greatest subtlety, until—flop! the whole thing comes apart like a clod of earth crumbling to the ground.

Orizaba takes you down to a terrible intersection. You need to cross Sagamore and both lanes of Alemany Boulevard—just at the point where Brotherhood Way merges into it. Luckily, there is a traffic island midway to take refuge in. This would be a great place for a bicycle overpass! After crossing over all the madness, turn left onto Alemany and proceed through the underpass below the 280 freeway. As soon as you're through, turn right onto tiny Crystal Street.

In 1 block you'll see DeLong Street, which curves around a residential neighborhood to arrive shortly at the Daly City BART station. If you intend to continue riding Part III, however, make a left onto Goethe Street and continue following the directions in Part III.

Ring around the City
Part III

Number of miles:	18.5
Approximate pedaling time:	2 hours
Terrain:	Hilly
Traffic:	Moderate
Things to see:	Mt. San Bruno State Park, Bayview Park, 3 Com Park, Third Street, South Park, Bay Bridge anchorage, Embarcadero, Ferry Building

This ride starts at the Daly City BART station and ends at the Ferry Terminal, where Part I starts. It includes a long, gradual climb and a short, steep one and offers outstanding views of San Francisco, the peninsula, the bay, and the ocean.

From the BART station turn left onto DeLong Street. When you get to Goethe Street, turn right. *Be watchful* of traffic as you cross busy San Jose and turn right onto Mission Street. In 1 block turn left onto Crocker Avenue.

Once you're on Crocker, the traffic is behind you and you can take a deep breath. In fact, you may want to take lots of deep breaths, as Crocker ascends steeply for the next half-dozen blocks.

Eventually Crocker levels out. After you pass Roosevelt Avenue, note a path on the right that meanders through Edgewood Park before dropping down to Daly City.

Continue on Crocker. Look for a trailhead on the right where a paved bike path begins. Go around the gate and continue on this beautiful path, which features lush ivy, wild fennel, and eucalyptus and bay trees, making for idyllic riding and lots of nice smells. After a mile cross a service road and continue straight on. When the path

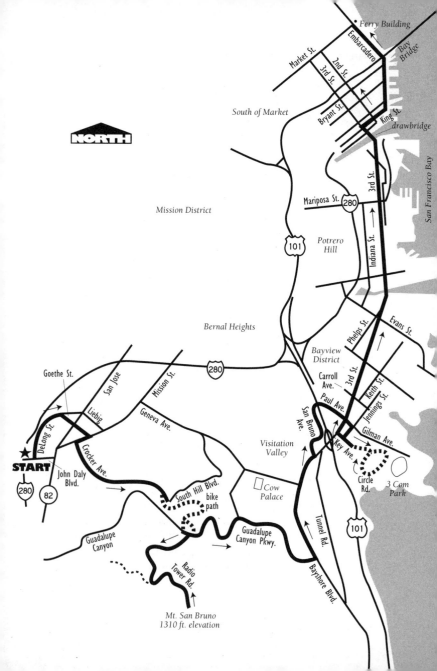

NORTH

Ferry Building

Bay Bridge

Market St.

2nd St.

3rd St.

Embarcadero

South of Market

Bryant St.

King St. drawbridge

Mission District

Mariposa St.

280

3rd St.

101

Potrero Hill

Indiana St.

San Francisco Bay

Bernal Heights

Evans St.

Phelps St.

Bayview District

280

Goethe St.

San Jose

Mission St.

Carroll Ave.

3rd St.

Keith St.

Liebig

Geneva Ave.

Paul Ave.

San Bruno Ave.

Jennings St.

Gilman Ave.

DeLong St.

Crocker Ave.

Key Ave.

Visitation Valley

Circle Rd.

3 Com Park

START

280

82

John Daly Blvd.

South Hill Blvd. bike path

Cow Palace

Guadalupe Canyon Pkwy.

Tunnel Rd.

101

Guadalupe Canyon

Radio Tower Rd.

Bayshore Blvd.

Mt. San Bruno 1310 ft. elevation

DIREC-TIONS at a glance

0.0	Start at Daly City BART; turn left onto DeLong Street.
0.3	Turn right onto Goethe Street.
0.4	Cross San Jose.
0.5	Turn right onto Mission Street.
0.6	Turn left onto Crocker Avenue.
1.8	Turn right onto paved bike path.
3.7	Path ends; turn right onto another path.
3.8	Drop onto Radio Tower Road and go through underpass.
5.5	Turn around at summit.
7.2	Go back through underpass.
7.3	Turn left past guard station on entrance road.
7.4	Turn left onto Guadalupe Canyon Parkway.
9.6	Turn left onto Bayshore Boulevard.
11.1	Turn left onto San Bruno Avenue (at 7-Eleven).
12.0	Turn right onto Paul Avenue.
12.4	Cross Third Street; Paul becomes Gilman Avenue.
12.5	Turn right onto Jennings Street.
12.7	Turn left onto Key Avenue.
12.8	Continue past gate.
13.0	Turn right onto Circle Road.
13.5	Turn right back onto path to Key.
13.7	Turn right onto Third Street.
18.0	Turn right onto King Street.
18.5	Turn left onto Embarcadero to finish at Ferry Building.

dead ends, turn right. Soon you'll come to an underpass where you can drop down off the curb onto Radio Road and begin the 1⁷⁄₁₀ mile climb to the summit. Near the top another path to the right leads out along a dinosaur tail–like ridge, with dramatic views to either side. There are private property signs stenciled on the path, but many local maps list it as a bicycle path—use your judgment.

If Mt. San Bruno were inside the city limits, it would easily be our tallest hill, but because it is slightly south of the border, that honor falls to Mt. Davidson. Radio Tower Road ultimately climbs up to 1,315 feet above sea level, plenty high enough to get a great view. Too often, however, the view is diminished by bad air quality, especially to the east. Aren't you glad you aren't adding to that brown layer?

Head back down the hill. After coasting back through the underpass, you'll get to test the geometric theorem that although two wrongs don't make a right, three lefts do. Turn left through the parking lot, left onto the service road past the guard station, and left onto Guadalupe Canyon Parkway.

Start heading east, down the hill, toward the bay. The parkway has a nice wide shoulder and is a good place to practice your speed tuck. Stay tucked until it ends on Bayshore and hang a left.

Take Bayshore 1½ miles north through industrial Brisbane, where firewood and cinderblock supply houses line the road. There are even a couple of statuary stores that have led Brisbane to be nicknamed "Northern Tijuana."

Past the statues, when Bayshore begins climbing and curving right, look for a 7-Eleven on the left and make a left onto San Bruno Avenue. San Bruno climbs and bends right, then left. As you near the top, note Candlestick Hill straight ahead. The next portion of the ride heads up to Bayview Park atop it.

Continue on San Bruno as it fronts the 101 freeway and begins to descend. San Bruno is the main drag of the Portola/University Mound neighborhood, but most of the activity can be found just past where our route turns right, which is on Paul Avenue.

Paul crosses under the freeway before crossing Bayshore Boulevard and Third Street. On the other side of Third, you'll find that Paul Street has changed names to Gilman Avenue. Make the first right off

Gilman onto Jennings Street. Climb 4 blocks and make a left onto Key Avenue.

At the top of Key, go around a gate and begin climbing up to Bayview Park. The path becomes a little bit steep here. Well, to be honest, it becomes brutally steep. Don't worry, though; your endorphins will only enhance the extremely great view from up top.

The path ends on a circular road that offers a series of breathtaking perspectives of the city and bay. Of San Francisco's many hilltop parks, Bayview is my favorite. After a circuit or two, go back down the path, down Key Avenue, and make a right onto Third Street.

There are plans to construct an electric trolley line on Third Street. During construction, or if lane width for bicycles decreases afterward, try the alternate route shown on the map. Otherwise, take Third all the way back to town.

After crossing the Lefty O'Doul bascule bridge, make the second right, onto King Street. King soon curves around to become Embarcadero, which in turn takes you back to the Ferry Building, where the ride began.

The broad promenade along the Embarcadero was christened Herb Caen Way in 1997 just before the great columnist died. It passes the mooring spot of the *Jeremiah O'Brian,* a restored liberty ship, which can be rented for parties and events. There's a nice grocery store at Brannan, just before you pass under the massive West Anchorage of the Golden Gate Bridge. After you've done all three parts of this ride, you can definitely say you've been around—the city, at least. So, did you learn anything?

Golden Gate Park

Number of miles:	9.6
Approximate pedaling time:	1 hour
Terrain:	Flat
Traffic:	Light
Things to see:	McLaren Lodge, Conservatory of Flowers, Rhododendron Dell, Music Concourse, de Young Museum, California Academy of Sciences, Asian Art Museum, Redwood Grove, Stow Lake, Pioneer Cabin, Speedway Meadows, Polo Fields, Buffalo Paddock, Chain of Lakes, Dutch Windmill, Queen Wilhelmina Tulip Garden, Cliff House, Beach Chalet, Ocean Beach, Hagiwara Tea Garden, Shakespeare Garden, Children's Playground, Hippie Hill

Golden Gate Park is one of the world's great landscaping feats. It has a long and fascinating history, if you like that sort of thing. It is also a bicycling center, virtually surrounded by bike shops, full of bike paths, and, on weekends, full of riders of all stripes.

This ride does a big loop around the park, taking in only a few of the great park's attractions. The route sheet won't do much good, since there are no street signs. In order to follow the route, you'll have to pay close attention to the map. You'll probably get lost anyway. But that's okay, for reasons that will become clear later.

Begin at McLaren Lodge, former home of John McLaren and still park headquarters. McLaren supervised Golden Gate Park for fifty-six

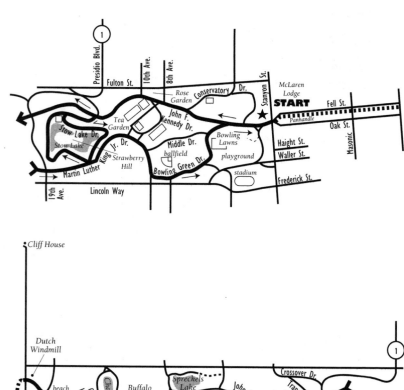

DIREC-TIONS at a glance

0.0   Begin at McLaren Lodge, in Golden Gate Park near intersection of Stanyon, Fell, and Oak streets. Ride west on John F. Kennedy Drive.

1.1   Turn left onto Stow Lake Drive, circle Stow Lake clockwise, and return to JFK Drive.

2.5   Turn left onto JFK Drive.

2.9   Turn left onto Transverse Road just past underpass.

2.94 Turn right into small lot and continue around gate on Overlook Drive.

3.24 Merge right onto Middle Drive.

3.7   Turn right on path to Polo Field just after Metson Road merges from the left. Follow path briefly right, then left through tunnel entrance to Polo Field.

3.8   Turn right onto paved bicycle track around Polo Field.

4.18 Ride halfway around track, turn right, and exit through tunnel on the opposite side, then left to JFK.

4.3   Turn left onto JFK Drive.

5.0   Turn right at T intersection to stay on JFK Drive.

5.4   Cross Great Highway and turn left onto Esplanade.

5.9   Recross Great Highway and continue on Lincoln Way.

6.0   Turn left onto Martin Luther King Jr. Drive and continue back into the park.

8.6   Turn left onto Bowling Green Drive.

9.2   Turn right onto Middle Drive.

9.3   Turn right onto JFK Drive.

9.6   End at McLaren Lodge.

years before passing on to greener pastures—if such may be imagined—at the age of ninety-six. An autocratic, cagey, rough-talking Scot with a thick burr, "Uncle John" was a beloved old San Francisco character. The large Monterey cypress in front of the lodge is strung with colored lights every December. A few old-timers still call it Uncle John's Christmas Tree.

McLaren inherited control of the park from William Hammond

Hall, who was, at age twenty-four, the first park superintendent. Hall is to be credited with grading the roaming, dry "great sand park" into undulating meadows rimmed by low hills planted into windbreaks, but McLaren turned the park into the pinnacle of landscape gardening that it is today.

Just past McLaren Lodge, stay right on John F. Kennedy Drive as busy Kezar Drive sweeps away to the left. On Sundays and holidays you'll have to ride around the barriers that close this section of the park to cars.

Soon you'll see the stunning white Conservatory of Flowers building on the right, set amid manicured flower gardens and encircled by trees. A great windstorm damaged the century-old Victorian greenhouse in 1996, and it may yet be closed, awaiting repairs.

Just past the conservatory a short street leads to the right. Here, skaters often dance on Sundays to loud music, and crowds of onlookers gather to watch.

To the left you'll notice the Rhododendron Dell, a tribute to McLaren's favorite plants. A side trip may be taken by bicycle along the circuitous paved and gravel paths here, although signs warn that no sport riding will be tolerated. If you like rhododendrons, you should seek out the Kruse Rhododendron Dell just north of Bodega Bay on the coast. Go there in late May.

People have ridden the bridle paths and running tracks of the park ever since the bicycle was invented. The mountain-bike boom has increased trail riding to the point where park officials have considered enforcing the statutes against "scorchers" on these paths. The main problem is not user conflicts, which have been relatively few, but the creation of new trails. If you ride the trails of the park, please stick to established routes. We don't want erosion to turn the park back into sand, now, do we? And ask at one of the shops around the park how to get involved in volunteer trail-maintenance programs.

Just ahead a left turn leads to the music concourse and the various museums that surround it. The depressed garden was put in for the California Midwinter Fair of 1894, and in 1899 sugar magnate Adolph Spreckels gave the city the music pavilion. You may wish to circle around the concourse plaza—noting in turn the de Young Museum, Asian Art Museum, and the California Academy of Sciences—before returning to John F. Kennedy Drive, going left, and continuing. Actually, the Asian Art Museum will soon move to the old downtown library building.

A tenth of a mile later the redwood grove begins on the right. If you wish to experience the cathedral-like grandeur here, walk your bike down the dirt road on the corner just past a small street to the right. Here are examples of California's famous coastal redwoods, capable of reaching heights of more than 300 feet. Some cyclists have made swooping paths with jumps here, a practice frowned upon by the park's caretakers, who occasionally position piles of brush and litter—or even fences—to discourage such use.

A bit farther down JFK, note the Rose Garden on the right. Then, in another ¼ mile, make a left on the road heading to Stow Lake. Pass the pioneer cabin on the left, and take the first left onto a one-way street that makes a clockwise circle around Stow Lake, the main water reservoir serving the substantial irrigation needs of the park.

When the road merges with Martin Luther King Jr. Drive, keep right, and then make another right soon after to continue circling the lake. Pass the lake's lodge, which offers refreshments as well as bike, boat, and surrey rentals. Continue back to JFK and turn left.

After you pass below an overpass, make a left onto Transverse Drive, climbing a short hill. At the top turn right onto Overlook Drive, past a car barrier that closes this beautiful lane to automobiles.

Incidentally, road racers meet here in front of the gate on Tuesdays and Thursdays during summer between 5:00 and 6:30 P.M. for a training ride that circles past this point. All levels of riders are present, and the roads are open to cars, baby carriages, and the occasional family of geese. Still, through the years, such noted racers as Laura Charameda, Roberto Gaggioli, Glen Winckle, J. P. Morgen, and Tom Weisel have taken part, and crashes have actually been remarkably few.

After riding around the gate, continue down Overlook Drive. Stay right where a road to the left leads to a park maintenance station. This is one of the park's best places to feel as though you're miles away from the city, with views of the old Speedway Meadows to the right and eucalyptus and bay trees to the left.

Speedway Meadows, once a horse-race track, is noteworthy as the site of the Human Be-In/Gathering of the Tribes, which effectively launched the hippie movement far out into the national consciousness. Acid had been made illegal some months before (on October 6, 1966—easy to remember because of the three 6s), so the publicized purpose of the Be-In was merely for people to dig one another. But those turkey sandwiches the Diggers passed out were garnished with more than mayonnaise.

A quarter-mile farther, Overlook merges back with Middle Drive, and a little bit beyond, with Metson Road. Just keep right and keep heading west and slightly downhill. Just past the merge with Metson Road, take a right onto a small paved path leading down through a tunnel to the old velodrome around the polo fields.

Ride halfway around and exit the track on the other side, through another tunnel. Swing left, past the Golden Gate Park Riding Academy, to where the road dead-ends at Spreckels Lake, port of call for many a radio-controlled miniature yacht. Make a left back onto JFK, which temporarily splits into one-way streets. *Be careful* not to turn onto the wrong half of the road! If you see a water fountain to the right, you're all right. Next, follow the sign to the beach—not Thirty-fifth Avenue—and you'll stay left on JFK as it merges back into two-way traffic.

Soon after, note the buffalo paddock on the right, where the great hairy brown behemoths have dwelled in fog- and mange-shrouded isolation since the late nineteenth century.

Soon you'll pass lakes to the left and right. In one of these the great San Francisco romantic poet George Sterling is said to have swum at midnight to fetch a lily his ladyfriend unwittingly admired. On another, later, occasion the Bohemian bard is said to have been caught dipping by a wandering constabulary. Although Sterling claimed to have a special dispensation—granted him as San Francisco poet emeritus, mind you—to take the Chain of Lakes waters at will, the cop was unimpressed and hauled the alcoholic poet downtown to dry out.

Past the lake on the right, continue straight through an intersection with Chain of Lakes Drive. A ¼ mile farther, make a right to stay on JFK Drive. Be wary of random balls flying through the trees from Golden Gate Park Golf Course to the right, or from the soccer fields to the left.

In another ¼ mile you'll pass the lovely Dutch windmill and Queen Wilhelmina Tulip Garden, a bit of wonderment at the height of its powers in spring. The windmill was built in 1902 to pump irrigation water from an underground river. A few years later, another was built at the southwestern edge of the park. For years these mills supplied all the park's water needs, but they were retired when the city purchased its water supply from private companies.

When you come to the Great Highway, cross over it and ride up to the ocean wall for a look out at the Pacific. A hardy contingent of surfers can usually be seen here plying the cold and undertowed waves. To the right, up the hill, you'll see the mighty Cliff House atop its fortresslike footing of rock.

If you have the time, there are a few good things to check out at the Cliff House: the Museé Mécanique, full of antique coin-operated amusements and passport photo booths; the Camera Obscura, a great place to look for the "green flash" at sunset on clear days; oysters on the half-shell; but I digress.

Looking toward the park from the ocean wall you'll see the Beach Chalet, designed by prominent architect Willis Polk. After standing empty for many years, the Beach Chalet was reopened in 1996 as a restaurant and microbrewery. Murals inside show Californians at play. They were painted by WPA artists during the 1930s and complement similar WPA art inside Coit Tower and the Rincon Annex Post Office at Mission and Spear, which portray Californians at work.

Back down at Ocean Beach, head south, with the ocean on the right. Ride ⁹⁄₁₀ mile and turn left onto Lincoln Way. If you want to extend your ride, pick up the biking/skating/baby carriage–pushing path that heads south just inland from the Great Highway. Follow it out until it ends at Sloat, in about 2 miles; then return.

Another option would be to turn right on La Playa (the next street up from the Great Highway) and follow it 2 blocks to Java Beach, among the all-time great 1990s-style coffeehouses in San Francisco. It has a bike rack and couches.

If you're ready for the trip back through the park, though, turn left from Lincoln at the first opportunity, riding back into the park on Martin Luther King Jr. Drive. Continue on MLK Drive for 1½ miles and continue past its intersection with Crossover Drive (Route 1). A half-mile farther, pass by an entrance on the right to Strybing Arboretum and Botanical Gardens, where footpaths closed to bicycles lead past gardens bearing myriad varieties of carefully labeled vegetable matter. Just past there, a one-way (wrong way) left-hand turn leads to the Hagiwara Japanese Tea Garden and the Shakespeare Garden, both within easy walking distance from the road.

The bust locked in a case at the far end of the Shakespeare Garden is one of only two copies made from an actual mask struck of old Billy Jigglejavelin; unfortunately the case is opened only on special occasions and by appointment.

Although small, the Tea Garden can provide for many hours of exploration. Established by George Turner Marsh for the Midwinter Fair of 1894, it was then taken over by Makoto Hagiwara and his family, who lived in a house on the premises, ran the teahouse, and created the garden over the course of nearly fifty years.

When Japan bombed Pearl Harbor the Hagiwaras were removed to a detention camp, and their house was bulldozed. Only in the 1970s did the city decide to formally recognize the Hagiwara's "gift" of the garden to the city and apologize for its crime. The family was invited to attend the laying of a bronze plaque in their honor, which they did. A picture of them that ran in the *Chronicle* spoke of poignant bitterness.

Returning to MLK Jr., go left. Pass up the next two chances to turn left, continuing on until you see a stoplight ahead on busy Lincoln Way. A hundred yards before the stoplight, turn left to stay on MLK. Soon you'll pass two baseball diamonds in a big field to the left. Take the next left, onto Bowling Green Drive, and head past an entrance to the children's playground, supposed to be the first public playground in the United States, dating back to 1887. Of particular note is the carousel, in which lovingly restored antique carved animals bob around to calliope tunes.

Next, you'll pass by the neatly groomed lawn-bowling grounds, where senior citizens in white suits gently roll their small spheres back and forth.

At the next intersection make a right back onto Middle Drive, passing the tennis courts on the right. At the stop sign make another right onto JFK Drive, where you can leave the park in the same place you entered it.

Or, if you want just one more side trip, ride over to the bike path on the right side of the road. Follow it as it curves to the right, and make two more right turns until you find yourself in a big open lawn—Sharon Meadows—with a grass-covered knoll to the right. This hill came to be known as Hippie Hill and was the site of many a drug-induced reverie and free-love session in the 1960s. On sunny weekend days lots of people lie out here. When ready, retrace your way to JFK and McLaren Lodge, where the tour began.

There are, of course, many attractions in Golden Gate park not visited by this ride. Your favorite places may well be those you discover in the course of your own explorations. One of the original ambitions of Hall and those who designed the park was to produce, with curving streets and a maze of meadows surrounded by view-obstructing trees, an area where, despite the limitations of physical space, a person could feel lost, as if in the actual wilderness. Hence the lack of street signs. While my hope is that you haven't gotten lost following my route, perhaps another time you'll appreciate a less structured experience in the further corners of this precious urban resource.

Useful Phone Numbers

Conservatory of Flowers: (415) 771–0280
Asian Art Museum: (415) 668–8921
California Academy of Sciences: (415) 750–7155
M. H. de Young Memorial Museum: (415) 750–3659 or 750–3600
McLaren Lodge: (415) 666–7200
Strybing Arboretum: (415) 661–1316 or (415) 558–3622

Midtown Mosey

Number of miles:	5.1
Approximate pedaling time:	30 minutes
Terrain:	Flat
Traffic:	Mostly light
Things to see:	Panhandle, Alamo Square, postcard views of downtown and Victorian architecture, City Hall, Main Library, Davies Symphony Hall, Opera House, Union Square

This route is about the flattest, mellowest ride there is from midtown to downtown. It begins in Golden Gate Park, near the intersection of Stanyan and Fell/Oak. Look for the bicycle path that runs through the Panhandle and take it east. It has a little yellow stripe down the middle, just like a miniature bicycle freeway.

In the Panhandle you'll find some of the city's oldest trees, planted at a time when high society came here on holidays and weekends to see and be seen, parading around in horse-drawn carriages. Gossip sections of the old newspapers refer often to the goings-on here. At that time, of course, the Panhandle was considered way out in the country.

In the late 1950s an extension of the 101 freeway was proposed through the Panhandle, but resident committees spearheaded by Jack Morrison successfully opposed the plan. Rents fell as a result—the neighborhood was suddenly too far out of town to be truly desirable. Low rents then paved the way for an influx of low- and no-income hippies who, during the "Summer of Love," took the Haight Ashbury even farther out.

During the hippie era the Panhandle was host to free Grateful

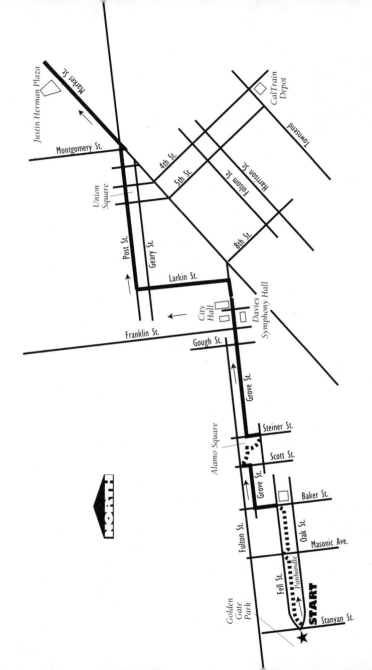

DIRECTIONS at a glance

0.0 Start at the bike path through the Panhandle, between Fell and Oak at Stanyan, heading east, away from Golden Gate Park.
0.5 Cross Masonic Avenue.
0.8 Left onto Baker Street.
1.0 Turn right onto Grove Street.
1.3 Turn left onto Scott Street.
1.4 Turn right onto bike path at corner into Alamo Square.
1.6 Exit opposite corner of park, and turn left onto Steiner Street.
1.7 Turn right onto Grove Street.
2.5 Turn left onto Larkin Street.
3.1 Turn right onto Post Street.
4.3 Right onto Montgomery Street, then immediately left onto Market Street.
5.1 End at Justin Herman Plaza.

Dead, Jefferson Airplane, and Janis Joplin concerts. The Diggers, who ran the Free Store, passed out free food that sometimes had interesting garnishes. There were happenings. Be-ins. Love-ins. Lots more fun than a freeway. If you are interested in touring around places of hippie history, pick up Stanus Fluoride's Hippie Map, an excellent poster-type guide available at many shops on Haight Street.

At Masonic Avenue signs stenciled on the pavement have pictographs of cars and warn of DEATH MONSTERS AHEAD. The path is interrupted by a traffic light but continues on the other side.

At Baker Street the path ends. Across the street, on a site once occupied by a velodrome, stands the Department of Motor Vehicles. At this point, turn left and take the bike lane onto Baker.

A few blocks farther you can turn right onto Grove Street to pick up another bike path. When it ends on Alamo Square, turn left onto Scott Street and ride 1 block to Fulton Street.

Fulton used to be four lanes wide, but now that it's only three there's a nice wide shoulder, at least between Masonic and downtown.

There's also a nice new bike path on Fulton (thanks, SFBC!). Grove Street also has an officially signed bike lane, but I think most people will prefer Fulton for transportation purposes, as it's faster and uninterrupted. Grove is good for moseying, though.

Since we're moseying, at the corner of Scott and Fulton, make a hard right into Alamo Square on the signed bike route that traverses the historic square.

Alamo Square was once a center of international diplomacy, with embassies built all around the hilltop park. At present the area is a historic district, and many of the buildings nearby, especially those on the north side, are worth taking a look at.

Today, the embassies are long gone. Tourists still flock here by the millions, however. Immense tour buses can nearly always be seen disgorging or collecting purses and wallets with large polyester-wearing people attached. They come to take pictures of "postcard row," the series of so-called painted ladies on Steiner Street, which, from the top edge of the park, appear to be turning their backs on the modern downtown world of the skyscrapers behind them.

Following the bike route signs through Alamo Square, you'll arrive diagonally at Hayes and Steiner. Up the hill on Hayes is the place to get the "postcard row" view. This is where the buses park, so that the tourists can get their painted lady shot, if they like, from the climate-controlled comfort of the bus itself. Grove Street, on which the route continues, picks up again ½ block down the hill on Steiner.

Grove then proceeds through the southern Western Addition, an area devastated by urban renewal programs during the 1960s and 70s, when tenement housing replaced many elegant but dilapidated Carpenter's Gothic Victorians. Some buildings appear quite new. HUD programs displaced thousands of African-Americans from lots that then stood empty—some for twenty years—before low-income housing programs were finally implemented.

Straight ahead, the verdigris (oxidized copper) dome of City Hall is visible. Soon, on the right, you'll see the glass curtains of Davies Symphony Hall, a goldfish bowl where the scales are musical.

When you see Davies on the right, look on the left side of the street and note the War Memorial Opera House, where the charter of the United Nations was signed in 1945, after World War II.

After crossing busy Van Ness Avenue, the through-town alignment of US 101, you'll pass by City Hall. As mentioned elsewhere, it is an exact replica of the Capitol building in Washington, except 17½ feet taller, perhaps a reminder to Washington that without California gold, the Civil War might have come out differently.

If you're heading to the South of Market district, keep straight on Grove, cross Market, and you can continue on Eighth Street. From there make a left onto Folsom Street or a right onto Harrison Street. A nice route to the CalTrain Depot is shown on the map: From Eighth Street turn left onto Folsom Street, then right onto Fifth Street, and then left onto Townsend Street for 1 block.

If heading downtown, follow the main route and make a left onto Larkin Street and continue up to Post Street. A right there will take you to Union Square, the true "civic center" of the city, the heart of the shopping and working districts. A few blocks beyond that, you'll arrive at Market Street and the Montgomery BART station.

One last note: If you wind up riding Fulton instead of Grove—as suggested earlier, Fulton is faster for commuting—make a right when you get to Gough Street, then a left onto Grove. Otherwise, you'll be forced into a series of left turns. Also, if traveling a significant distance north—say, to North Beach—you may prefer taking Franklin Street, a bicycle-friendly street 1 block west of Van Ness.

There you have it. The Midtown Mosey. May be ridden forward or backward by substituting Geary Boulevard for Post Street and Polk for Larkin. Scenic things along the way. With the Fulton Street, non-moseying option thrown in. A short but agreeable route. Hope you enjoy it, and find it useful.

Oh, and about that painted lady photo-op spot? Buy the postcard. It's easier.

Haight to Golden Gate

Number of miles:	4 one-way, 8 round-trip
Approximate pedaling time:	30 minutes
Terrain:	Flattest possible route
Traffic:	Light except for Arguello Boulevard
Things to see:	A corner of Golden Gate Park, including the Conservatory of Flowers, the Columbarium, Presidio National Park, Golden Gate Bridge

This route travels from Haight Street, near the geographic center of San Francisco, to the Golden Gate Bridge on a popular route that always has a steady flow of bicycle traffic, especially on sunny weekend days. Although mostly a connecting route to rides across the Golden Gate Bridge, it is scenic in itself since it links up Golden Gate Park and Presidio National Park, two popular in-town riding areas.

Begin at the intersection of Haight and Stanyan Street, at the easternmost edge of Golden Gate Park. This area is a small mecca of bike shops. There are several within a few blocks that rent bikes.

Begin riding north on Stanyan, as though you had just made a right from Haight. After passing Page Street you need to turn left onto John F. Kennedy Drive. Since a left turn here is illegal, go straight across this busy intersection and stop on the far side. Then, when the light has changed, proceed into the park on JFK Drive. A few hundred yards farther the road splits; stay right as Fell Street becomes Kezar Drive and wends leftward. Some people prefer to turn into the park on a bike path across from Page Street, wait at the traffic light on Kezar, turn right, and then left onto JFK.

After a tenth of a mile on JFK make a right onto East Conservatory Drive, a one-way road with a sign pointing to the Fuchsia Dell

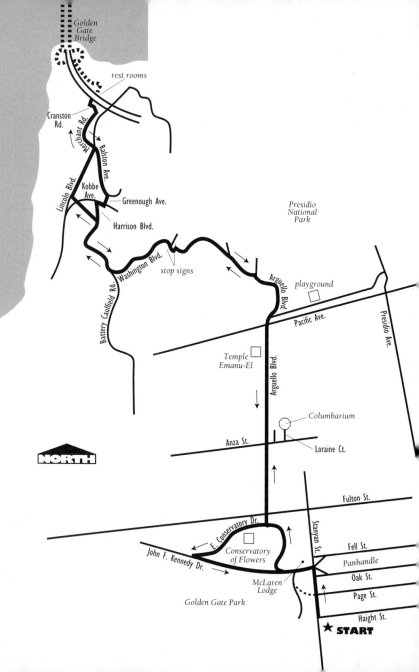

Golden Gate Bridge

rest rooms

Cranston Rd.

Merchant Rd.

Ralston Ave.

Lincoln Blvd.

Kobbe Ave.

Greenough Ave.

Harrison Blvd.

Battery Caulfield Rd.

Washington Blvd.

stop signs

Presidio National Park

Arguello Blvd.

playground

Pacific Ave.

Presidio Ave.

Temple Emanu-El

Arguello Blvd.

Columbarium

Anza St.

Loraine Ct.

NORTH

Fulton St.

E. Conservatory Dr.

John F. Kennedy Dr.

Conservatory of Flowers

Stanyan St.

Fell St.

Panhandle

Oak St.

McLaren Lodge

Page St.

Golden Gate Park

Haight St.

★ **START**

DIREC-TIONS at a glance

0.0	Start at Stanyan and Haight streets.
0.1	Turn left into Park at John F. Kennedy Drive.
0.2	Turn right onto one-way East Conservatory Drive to Fuchsia Dell and Arguello Boulevard.
0.5	Turn right onto Arguello.
1.5	Enter Presidio. Follow Arguello as it curves to right.
1.8	Turn left onto Washington Boulevard.
2.4	Stay left at stop sign.
2.7	Pass Battery Caulfield Road.
3.1	Stay left on Washington.
3.2	Stop sign at Kobbe Avenue; stay straight.
3.3	Merge with Lincoln Boulevard.
3.5	Turn left onto Merchant Road.
3.6	Turn left onto Cranston Road.
3.7	Go right, through underpass.
3.7	Take immediate left after underpass up bike path.
4.0	End at Golden Gate Bridge.

and Arguello Boulevard. Follow it as it climbs and curves to the left. Then, at the first intersection, make a right and coast down a short hill to Fulton Street, which borders Golden Gate Park to the north. When the light is green, cross Fulton and continue on Arguello Boulevard.

If you feel like checking out an interesting building, make a right onto Anza Street and take the second left onto Loraine Court. There you'll see the octagonal Columbarium, once part of an extensive group of cemeteries moved to Colma, south of San Francisco, in 1901 to allow the city to expand west of Divisadero Street. The Columbarium has niches for the ashes of 25,000, and, being made entirely of stone, metal, and glass, is itself incapable of burning. The building is open regularly for visiting hours and offers services that sometimes include Asian language chants.

Back on Arguello, continue north past a large synagogue, Temple

Emanu-El, on the left. Continue on Arguello until the road steepens sharply and you pass between the gates of the Presidio, founded in 1776 and proclaimed a national park in 1994.

Presidios were established near many California missions to protect Spain's interests in the New World. The one in San Francisco, despite being ruled by three different governments—Spain, Mexico, and the United States—in various times of inter- and intranational strife, has never seen any combat action. In fact, most of the bloodshed here through the years probably occurred during the aptly named Flying Wheels Criterium, held annually in March—when novice road racers are at their sketchiest—in an absurdly cramped parking lot down near the Marina.

After passing through the gates, continue on Arguello as it swings around to the right. Arguello was named for Don Luis Arguello, a native San Franciscan who served as the first governor of California under Mexican rule.

When the road forks, make a left onto the high road, Washington Boulevard. Shortly thereafter stay left again on Washington. Soon you'll come to a stop sign. Although seemingly in the middle of nowhere, with clear visibility all around, lots of tickets used to be issued to cyclists here when the U.S. Army ruled the roost before national park days. Might as well continue an old tradition and come to an extra full stop here.

A half-mile farther you'll see Battery Caulfield Road to the left. This route leads downhill into and through the parking lot of the abandoned old Veterans Administration hospital building, which also once served as the U.S. Defense Language Institute, and out onto Fifteenth Avenue. Battery Caulfield is used by Richmond and Sunset riders to access the bridge.

Just past that, Central Magazine Road and Harrison Boulevard intersect Washington. Veer left to stay on Washington.

Next, you'll come to a stop sign at Kobbe Avenue. Go straight as Washington becomes a one-way street. Just beyond, merge with Lincoln Boulevard and continue downhill. Be on the lookout for the next left turn, onto Merchant Road.

Merchant, after curving left near an old army battery, brings you near all the traffic pouring over the Golden Gate Bridge. Just before reaching the bridge's roadway, turn left onto Cranston Road and drop down a short hill. Make a right into an underpass tunnel. When you emerge, make an immediate left onto the bike path that climbs up to the east sidewalk. There are rest rooms and a drinking fountain here, and it is a popular meeting spot for cyclists going riding together in Marin.

What you do next will be determined by the time and day of the week. The west sidewalk, reached via a path to the right that circles back under the bridge, is currently open from 7:00 A.M. to 9:00 P.M. on weekends and holidays, and weekdays from 3:30 to 9:00 P.M. It is the preferred route, as pedestrians are prohibited. At all other times of the day, it is necessary to share the east sidewalk with camera-wielding tourists, unpredictable joggers, and an occasional mainte-nance buggy. *Be cautious* and go slow.

After 9:00 P.M. cyclists can push a button near the gate that closes off the east sidewalk at night. The gate will open after a bridge sen-tinel in the toll plaza across the roadway has verified that you are a cyclist rather than a potential suicide. Show your appreciation for twenty-four-hour access to this important thoroughfare by waving to the gatekeeper behind the big plate-glass windows near the tollbooth.

No matter what time of day it is, and which sidewalk you ride on, go slow. You're not out of town yet! Riding the west sidewalk on a sunny weekend day is a perilous prospect, as lots of very inexperi-enced riders weave and dodge their way skitterishly across.

The metal plates on the bridge become extremely slippery when dampened by rain, mist, or even fog. Do not try to turn or brake while crossing these plates, especially those near the towers. The wind turbulence intensifies around the towers—*be extra careful* there.

In 1977 a couple of cyclists who crashed while riding around the towers sued the Bridge District, which reacted by closing the Golden Gate Bridge to all bicycle traffic. Public outcry ensued, and the clo-sure was rescinded, but not before signs had been installed admon-ishing cyclists to walk their bikes around the towers. Hardly anyone does this, however.

Don't spend all your bridge-crossing time worrying. Take time to contemplate the geographic significance here. The Golden Gate is the only break in a 400-mile barrier of coastal mountains separating California's long Central Valley from the Pacific. Forty percent of California's land area drains its freshwater flow here. Or would, if it weren't diverted to Los Angeles instead.

The Sacramento River, which drains Mt. Shasta, Mt. Lassen, and the northern Sierras, and the San Joaquin River, which flows from the massive southern Sierras, highest mountains in the continental United States, flow together near Pittsburg before entering the bay through the Carquinez Straits. The Port Costa Loop ride (Route 16) offers a scenic view of the Carquinez Straits.

Saltwater also flows into the bay twice a day as the tide rolls in. Hence, massive amounts of water pour in and out of the bay four times each day. After spring rains you can watch the muddy river water intermix with salty ocean water in kaleidoscopic patterns.

As for the bridge itself, it, too, is worth considering. At one time the world's longest suspension bridge, its planning began in 1916 and it was finished in 1937 at a cost of $35 million—and eleven lives. It came in on budget and on time despite unprecedented engineering problems. The south tower stands in a hundred feet of fast-moving water. The anchorages and piers contain enough concrete to build a 5-foot-wide sidewalk from San Francisco to New York. The cables are made up of ¼-inch-thick stainless-steel rod so strong that an 18-inch length of it was impossible for any of the men who built the bridge to bend. Some 80,000 miles of this cable, enough to wrap around the earth's equator three times, were spun on-site into the bridge cables. The towers are 746 feet above waterline, or about one-third as high as Mt. Tamalpais. They are constructed of hollow, modular 1-inch steel-walled box sections field-riveted together. During bridge construction an innovative safety net saved many lives; those who benefited from it became members of the Halfway to Hell club. Some cyclists who have survived a tumble over the low barriers into the traffic lanes consider themselves honorary members. Ten of the bridge's eleven fatalities during construction occurred when a platform hung underneath the roadway for form removal plunged to the water, ripping the safety net with it.

The return route back to the Haight is slightly different. After exiting the bridge sidewalk bike path past the toll-plaza gift shop, turn right, go through the underpass, and left up the hill on Cranston Road. Go right onto Merchant, and follow it up to Lincoln Boulevard. Instead of turning right onto Lincoln, though, cross over it and turn right onto Ralston Avenue, which runs behind a series of dormitory-style buildings. When Ralston begins to curve left, make a right onto Greenough Avenue, then the next right onto Kobbe Avenue. Then, make the first left onto Harrison Boulevard. Harrison takes you to Washington Boulevard, where you can make a left and retrace the route back to Golden Gate Park.

Once inside the park, another deviation is necessary. Enter the park on Arguello and climb a short block. But instead of going left on East Conservatory Drive—which is a one-way street—take it right as it circles behind the beautiful white Victorian Conservatory of Flowers before meeting John F. Kennedy Drive. Take a left onto JFK. When it intersects with Kezar Drive, merge right across this busy thoroughfare. Finally, go right onto Stanyan Street and back up to Haight Street. Stanyan is very narrow here—wait for a clear opportunity and *be careful*!

There you have it. After a while this route will become second nature to you, as it already is to thousands of San Francisco cyclists. Welcome to the Bridge Rider's club!

Sneaky Crosstown Route

Number of miles:	7.1
Approximate pedaling time:	30 minutes
Terrain:	Some steep hills
Traffic:	Minimal
Things to see:	Views, tiny scenic backways, Tank Hill, Market Street overpasses, San Jose Street bridges, Holly Park Circle, community garden, Faith Street overpass, Bayshore waterfront

This route is more than just another pretty face. Although one of the most scenic routes in this book, it is also highly useful—though little known—as a transportation route from the Haight to Bernal Heights, and to neighborhoods in between such as the Castro, Noe Valley, and the Outer Mission. After reaching Bernal Heights it continues up and over the hill to Bayshore Boulevard and Third Street.

It does involve some initial climbing, especially if ridden in reverse, but once it gains its altitude it follows a natural ridgeline to conserve elevation and shoot across town high above the flatter valley routes so dominated by automobile traffic. Good climbers will find it the fastest route to take from the Haight to many points south, and all will love this route for its sweeping vistas and secret alley–route charm.

From Haight and Cole streets, begin south on Cole. When it starts to get really steep, make a right onto Rivoli Street and then the next left onto Shrader Street. Go 2 blocks and make another left onto Carmel Street, which takes you up to Twin Peaks Boulevard, a busy street with fast traffic. Go right onto Twin Peaks, up the hill. After about a hundred yards, get in the left lane and turn left onto Villa Terrace, which looks more like a driveway than anything else.

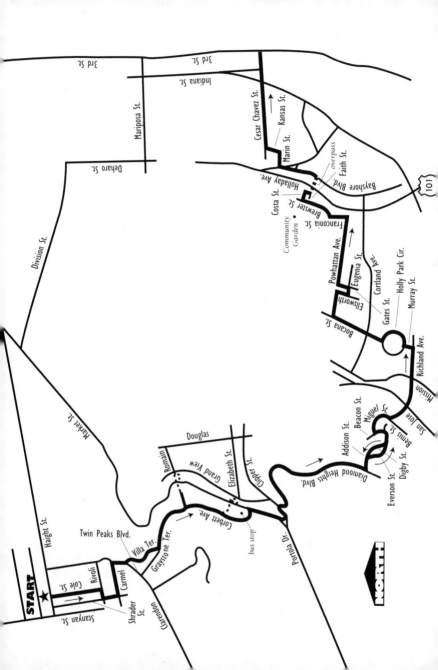

DIREC-TIONS at a glance

0.0	From Haight and Cole, head south on Cole, up the hill.
0.5	Turn right on Rivoli Street.
0.6	Turn left onto Shrader Street.
0.7	Turn left onto Carmel Street.
0.9	Turn right onto Twin Peaks Boulevard.
1.0	Turn left onto Villa Terrace.
1.2	Merge left with Graystone Terrace.
1.3	Merge right with Corbett Avenue.
1.8	Turn right onto Portola Drive.
2.1	Turn left onto Clipper Street.
2.2	Turn right onto Diamond Heights Boulevard.
2.9	Turn left onto Addison Street.
3.1	Turn right onto Everson Street.
3.3	Turn left onto Beacon Street.
3.4	Turn right onto Miguel Street.
3.9	Cross Mission Street; continue on Richland Avenue.
4.1	Turn left onto Murray Street; then right onto Holly Park Circle.
4.3	Turn right onto Bocana Street.
4.6	Turn right onto Powhattan Avenue.
4.8	Turn right onto Ellsworth Street.
4.9	Turn left onto Eugenia Street.
5.0	Turn left onto Gates Street.
5.1	Turn right onto Powhattan Street.
5.2	Turn left onto Franconia Street.
5.4	Continue right onto Brewster Street.
5.5	Turn right onto Costa Street.
5.6	Turn right onto Holladay Avenue; then left onto Faith Street overpass.
5.8	Turn right onto Bayshore Boulevard; make U-turn to go north.
6.1	Turn right onto Marin Street.
6.2	Turn left onto Kansas Street.
6.3	Turn right onto Cesar Chavez Street.
7.1	End at Third Street.

After a couple of blind corners (*go slow*), Villa crosses over the Pemberton stairs, some of the city's most picturesque. If you're a cyclocrosser, trot up and down them a couple of times. Note that Villa is a one-way street. If riding this route in reverse, walk your bicycle during this short stretch.

Pretty soon Villa merges into Graystone Terrace. Follow Graystone left as it wends around the contours of the hillside and merges into Corbett Road, where you make a right.

If your destination is Noe Valley, you can take either of two beautiful spiral pedestrian overpasses over Market Street. The first is found by turning left on Romain Street. The second is very hard to find. Look for a bus stop on the left with a well-hidden bike path behind it. Take this path down a short, steep hill. Be ready to brake because the path gets very steep just before it turns right and lets you out onto the dramatic arch across Market Street.

If you're not heading for Noe Valley, continue on the main route by following Corbett until it ends at Market. Make a right and climb for a short distance before making the next left onto Clipper Street. Then take an immediate right onto Diamond Heights Boulevard.

Take Diamond Heights Boulevard past the Safeway shopping center and look for the second left, Addison Street. Turn here and continue up a short, steep hill to Everson Street, where you make a right and find another dramatic overlook. Next, take the second left, onto Beacon Street, and then an immediate right onto Miguel Street.

Miguel plunges steeply down toward San Jose Avenue, which it passes over on an old bridge. For some reason, the view here of San Jose and the other bridges that cross it always reminds me of the bridges in Paris over the Seine. Okay, so maybe it ain't Pont Neuf.

The next busy street you come to is Mission Street, which must be crossed at ground level. Miguel has now changed into Richland Avenue, and should be taken uphill for another long block past Mission. When you get to Murray Street, make a left and then a right onto Holly Park Circle, one of San Francisco's loveliest hilltop parks. Look for Bocana Street, the fourth street around, and turn onto it.

You can now take Bocana up to Cortland Avenue, main street of the Bernal Heights district. You can follow Cortland up, over the hill, and down to Bayshore Boulevard, a commercial strip with giant businesses like Whole Earth Access, Goodman Lumber, carpet and tile shops, and other industrial supply houses.

If you prefer to take a scenic (read: hillier) route, continue on Bocana all the way to Powhattan Street and turn right. Students of history (or Disney movies) may recall that Powhattan founded a junta of several dozen Algonquian tribes in Virginia and was Pocahontas's father.

Follow tiny, scenic Powhattan until it dead-ends at Ellsworth Street. Turn right onto Ellsworth for 1 block; then turn left onto Eugenia Street, supposedly named for the pulchritudinous daughter of a San Bruno Road toll keeper in the early 1900s. Continue for 1 block before turning left onto Gates Street. Finally, turn right back onto Powhattan and continue until it dead-ends again. There, go left on Franconia Street and follow it as it veers right and becomes Brewster Street. Brewster Street was one of the last San Francisco streets to be paved. It happened in 1996 despite the objections of some residents. Soon you'll come to a lovely community garden on the left and Costa Street to the right. Take Costa 1 block down to Holladay Avenue, go right for 1 block to Faith Street, and look for the Faith Street overpass to the left.

Take this dramatic pedestrian overpass down to Bayshore Boulevard. Make a right, get in the left lane, and make a U-turn back up Bayshore. Continue on Bayshore as it approaches a hideous freeway interchange and take the last possible right onto Marin Street. Marin turns a corner near the KOFY radio station building and takes you to Cesar Chavez Street, where you can go right.

Cesar Chavez Street used to be called Army Street. It was renamed in the mid-1990s for the great labor leader who founded the United Farm Workers and organized the 1965 grape boycott. Cesar Chavez Street leads to Third Street, which you can turn left onto and take back into downtown San Francisco on a much flatter but much busier route.

Another option that is sneakier than the Third Street route is to turn left from Cesar Chavez Street onto Indiana Street. After 1 mile turn left onto Mariposa Street. In ½ mile turn right on DeHaro Street. A left on Division takes you up to Market Street.

Planet of the Apes Road

Number of miles:	17.4 one-way, 34.8 round-trip
Approximate pedaling time:	2–4 hours
Terrain:	Hilly, but not steep
Traffic:	Very light
Things to see:	SF Zoo, Lake Merced, Mussel Rock Park, Mori's Point, cool statue of Don Gaspar de Portolá, old rusty cars, McKnee Ranch State Park

This is a really fantastic ride! The people who already know about Planet of the Apes Road are going to be bummed out to see it in a guidebook, but I figure anyone cool enough to buy my book deserves to know.

Planet of the Apes Road is actually San Pedro Mountain Road, the old alignment of Highway 1 before Devil's Slide was built. It is now closed to car traffic since it runs through McKnee Ranch State Park. Overgrown and washed out in places, it is vaguely reminiscent of that final scene in *Planet of the Apes*—you expect to see the Statue of Liberty sticking up through the waves any second.

This route starts in San Francisco and takes back streets, many fronting the ocean, down to Linda Mar, where Planet of the Apes Road begins. This ride is best done as an overnight trip to the youth hostel near the lighthouse in Montara. Like all AYH youth hostels, it will never turn you away if you arrive on a bicycle. Still, be courteous and make a reservation: (415) 728–7177. Then get a few folks together and make a weekend of it.

Meet at the San Francisco Zoo, at the intersection of Sloat Boulevard and the Great Highway. Proceed up a slight hill before turning right onto Skyline Boulevard. After you pass John Daly Boulevard on

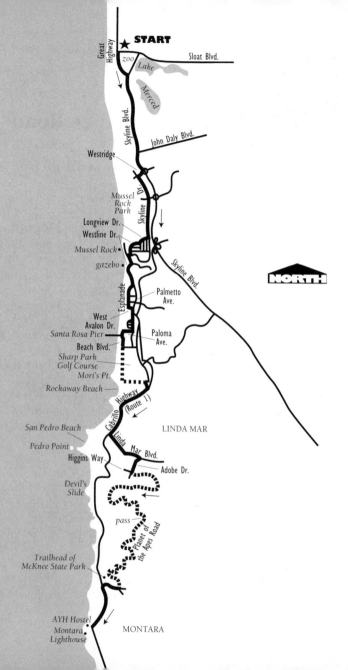

START

Great Highway

Sloat Blvd.

zoo

Lake Merced

Skyline Blvd.

John Daly Blvd.

Westridge

Skyline Dr.

Mussel Rock Park

Longview Dr.

Westline Dr.

Mussel Rock•

gazebo •

Skyline Blvd.

Esplanade

Palmetto Ave.

West Avalon Dr.

Santa Rosa Pier

Paloma Ave.

Beach Blvd.

Sharp Park Golf Course

Mori's Pt.

Rockaway Beach

Cabrillo Highway (Route 1)

LINDA MAR

San Pedro Beach

Pedro Point

Higgins Way

Linda Mar Blvd.

Adobe Dr.

Devil's Slide

pass

Planet of the Apes Road

Trailhead of McKnee State Park

AYH Hostel

Montara Lighthouse

MONTARA

NORTH

DIREC-TIONS at a glance

0.0	Start at Sloat Boulevard and Great Highway.
1.2	Turn right onto Skyline Boulevard.
1.6	Fort Funston parking lot on right.
2.4	Turn right onto Westridge, then left onto Skyline Drive.
5.2	Turn right onto Longview Drive.

5.4 Turn right onto Westline Drive.

5.8 Turn right onto Skyline Drive.

5.9 Turn left onto Westline Drive.

6.1 Turn right onto Palmetto Avenue.

6.5 Turn right onto Esplanade; check out gazebo.

7.3 Turn left onto West Avalon Drive.

7.4 Turn right onto Palmetto Avenue.

8.0 Turn right onto Paloma Avenue.

8.1 Turn left onto Beach Boulevard.

8.4 Go straight onto dirt road.

9.0 Road ends at cliff; turn left onto Mori's Point dirt road.

9.2 Turn right onto on-ramp.

9.3 Merge onto Cabrillo Highway (Highway 1).

11.5 Turn left onto Linda Mar Boulevard.

12.2 Turn right onto Adobe Drive.

12.6 Turn left onto Higgins Way.

12.7 Continue onto Planet of the Apes Road.

14.3 Cross powerline.

14.4 Top of climb.

14.7 Turn right onto wide dirt road.

14.8 Dirt road curves left; pavement resumes.

15.7 Turn right to stay on pavement.

16.2 Proceed through gate; turn right.

16.4 Turn left onto Highway 1.

17.4 Finish at AYH hostel, lighthouse on right.

the left, make the next right onto Westridge Avenue, then make a quick left onto Skyline Drive. If you're ready for a rest, continue straight on Westridge, which takes you to Palisades Park, a nice rest area.

Skyline Drive parallels Skyline Boulevard, climbing alongside it up to the top of Daly City Hill. Once up top, take a right onto Longview Drive and begin the steep descent to Mussel Rock. Look to the right where vacant lots present the opportunity and you may see paragliders, who often launch from the grassy terraces of Mussel Rock Park.

Soon you'll have to make a right onto Westline Drive, which plummets steeply down. At the base it intersects with Skyline Drive. Turn right. Skyline promptly dead-ends. To the right note the Mussel Rock garbage facility, where you can pay to leave your trash. There's. also a parking lot for Mussel Rock Park, where you'll find numerous trails, the aforementioned terraces, and, down near the ocean, big chunks of pavement, some still showing lane striping, which once constituted a coastal highway done in by the 1957 earthquake. There's that Planet of the Apes thing, again.

Also here, of course, is Mussel Rock, a medium-sized sea stack with an enormous diamond-shaped billboard-style reflector perched atop it. The geologic history of this particular "cowboy" is covered extensively in the first chapter of John McPhee's book *Assembling California*. Basically the rock is supposed to have ridden to its current location in the crevice between the two tectonic plates separated by the San Andreas fault.

After checking out the park, head south on the coast-front road, Westline Drive. When it ends on Palmetto Avenue, turn right. Make another right a bit farther, onto Esplanade. Here, as the road curves down a residential street, look on the right for a gazebo in front of a condo complex. This is a highly recommended stop. Past the gazebo are beautiful sandstone cliffs carved by the waves. At present there are no guardrails to mar the view. With sea stacks and cliffs like these it feels more like the Oregon than California coast. Esplanade soon ends on Avalon Drive. Go right. Next, turn right onto Palmetto.

Palmetto carries us into Sharp Park. As you ride into this cute little beach community, look for Paloma Avenue and make a right. Paloma carries you 1 block down to Beach Boulevard, where you go left along a seawall promenade often bustling with tourists and retirees. Halfway along the seawall a pier extends out into the ocean, but signs are posted prohibiting bicycles.

A little farther along an immense anchor is on display, a monument to the power of rust. Just past the anchor, continue on a good dirt levee road that separates the ocean from Sharp Park Golf Course. The lagoon to the left is called Laguna Salada.

The levee road is eventually blocked by the immense cliffs of Mori's Point. Turn left here onto Mori's Point Road, a dirt lane that runs past some fields and a residential neighborhood. Eventually it arrives at Highway 1, where our route turns right.

Highway 1 is fairly quiet south of Sharp Park, except on sunny weekend days. The shoulder is adequate. Take the bike path if you like or stay on the road.

If you really can't stand the idea of riding 2 miles on Highway 1, you might be able to scout a way through to Linda Mar Boulevard on the trails of Sweeney Ridge, an open space administered by the Golden Gate National Recreation Area that lies on the east side of 101. Besides excellent hiking and mountain biking trails, Sweeney Ridge contains the San Francisco Bay Discovery Site, where Don Gaspar de Portolá, on a scouting expedition, discovered San Francisco Bay. Ships had sailed, unheeding, past the Golden Gate for decades. How ironic that one of the world's great harbors was discovered by a land expedition!

After turning south onto Highway 1, be on the lookout for a historical monument, a large statue of Gaspar de Portolá on the left side of the road. The statue, a gift from Spain, portrays Portolá as a cross between Darth Vadar and Don Quixote. It's definitely worth stopping to stare at in amazement.

After passing the sleepy settlements of Vallemar and Rockaway Beach, you'll arrive in the somewhat blighted suburban town of Linda Mar. Here, turn left onto Linda Mar Boulevard, a busy road that climbs gently. After ¾ mile escape right onto Adobe Drive. A small liquor store/grocery here marks the last chance to buy food for a while.

When Adobe gets steep, look for a left onto Higgins Way, a short street that ends at the trailhead of Planet of the Apes Road. Ah! Planet of the Apes Road!

The car gate here, flanked by large-boled arboreal gateposts and cluttered with some big fallen logs, seems designed to keep out not just cars but anything or anybody less than spry. Navigating this entrance is worth the effort, though.

Planet of the Apes Road climbs gently through open space. The surface, once pavement, is now a bit scrofulous and littered and, in places, is completely washed away. There are a few sections you might have to walk around if you're on a road bike. Because the grades are gentle, you shouldn't have too much trouble managing on skinny tires, however.

After climbing for a little while, you'll cross under a gigantic powerline and over a few different strands of powerline road. Just stay straight on the pavement.

Just past the powerline, you'll pass through an odd steel-pipe gate. Look to the right here and you'll see the rusting carcasses of a few cars that missed Deadman's Curve when this trail was the main coastal highway.

Actually, this trail nearly became the main road again, due to the perennial landslides that close Devil's Slide. Instead, residents voted to build a tunnel. It remains to be seen what sort of consideration bicycles will be given to use the tunnel.

Continue as the path sidehills and descends gently. Soon you'll come to a bad washout. A bit farther on you'll emerge onto a wide, graded dirt road. Turn right and drop steeply down a short way before rejoining the paved surface of Planet of the Apes Road and continuing down to the left.

Many switchbacks and washouts make this a technical descent. There are several places where the road disappears without warning into washouts, often just past a blind curve. Although the view is phenomenal, *pay attention* to the road, too.

Near the bottom of the descent a dirt lane branches out to the left. Just stay right on the paved surface. You'll wind down a few more switchbacks before going past some abandoned bathtubs, through a gate, past someone's front yard, and taking a right onto a road that runs a short distance out to Highway 1.

Once on the highway turn left and head south to the lighthouse and nearby AYH Youth Hostel. Try to avoid dreaming about Roddy McDowall. Oh, and don't tell too many people about this ride.

Foster City Flats

Number of miles:	15.5
Approximate pedaling time:	90 minutes
Terrain:	Flat
Traffic:	Almost none
Things to see:	Airplanes taking off and landing, San Francisco Bay Trail, Coyote Point, marshlands, San Mateo Bridge, Foster City

There aren't many places in the Bay Area that are truly flat. This ride, however, skirts the bay, staying close down by the water, and for that reason, it is very flat. I mean, it is flat. We're talking flat. Friend, I said, "flat." Much of this ride consists of the San Francisco Bay Trail, a multiuse path that runs for many miles without so much as crossing over a street with auto traffic. So in addition to being flat, this ride is almost traffic-free.

This ride is scenic as well, with endless bay views and a couple of great airplane-watching spots. Perhaps best of all, except for freeway overpasses, there really are no hills whatsoever on this route. Did I mention this is a flat ride?

You can start this flat ride at San Francisco International Airport or from the Millbrae CalTrain station. Bikes are allowed in the northernmost cars of all CalTrains.

To get to the airport from San Francisco, follow SFO Ramble (Ride 15). When you get to the airport, instead of following signs to the terminal and turning left, continue straight on McDonnel and pick up the route from there.

If you take the CalTrain to the Millbrae stop, turn right out of the station onto Millbrae Avenue. Take Millbrae a few blocks, over a free-

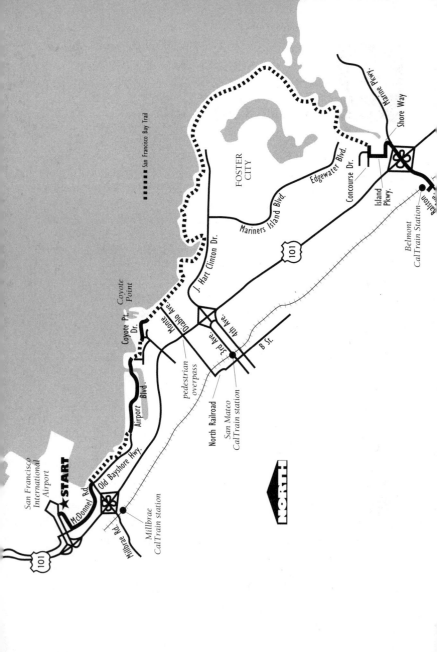

San Francisco Bay Trail

San Francisco
International
Airport

★ START

McDonnel Rd.

Old Bayshore Hwy.

Airport Blvd.

Millbrae Rd.

Millbrae
CalTrain station

101

Coyote
Point

Coyote Pt.
Dr.

Monte Diablo Ave.

pedestrian
overpass

North Railroad

San Mateo
CalTrain station

3rd Ave.

4th Ave.

B St.

J. Hart Clinton Dr.

Mariners Island Blvd.

FOSTER
CITY

101

Edgewater Blvd.

Concourse Dr.

Island
Pkwy.

Marine Pkwy.

Shore Way

Ralston

Belmont
CalTrain Station

NORTH

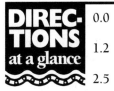

DIREC-TIONS at a glance

0.0	Start at San Francisco Airport, heading south on McDonnel Road.
1.2	Cross Millbrae; continue onto Old Bayshore Highway.
2.5	Old Bayshore ends. Turn left on sidewalk of Airport Boulevard; pick up San Francisco Bay Trail.
3.1	Path ends; turn left onto Airport Boulevard.
3.6	Cross bridge; note sidewheel steamer.
4.4	Pick up trail again on left.
5.0	Turn left into Coyote Point Drive.
5.1	Exit Coyote Point Drive onto San Francisco Bay Trail.
14.1	Continue straight onto Concourse Drive.
14.3	Turn left onto Island Parkway.
14.7	Turn right onto Marine Parkway.
15.0	Marine Parkway becomes Ralston Avenue.
15.3	Turn right onto El Camino Real.
15.5	Turn right into Belmont CalTrain station to finish.

way overpass, and onto the Bayshore Highway, where you go right and pick up the route. Look for a bike path along the bay, parallel to the Bayshore.

Shortly you'll come to a drinking fountain and a few fish-cleaning stations. You may want to stop here and clean any fish you happen to have with you. Or you might want to rest on one of the benches and watch the airplanes take off and land. Otherwise, continue along the path.

The path ends shortly, after less than a mile. You can either get back on Airport Boulevard and continue south or else continue south nearer to the bay, on a series of paved and unpaved paths.

Soon you'll cross a bridge where, to the left, you can see an old sidewheel steamer at anchor that was once a floating restaurant. Side-wheelers were common in the bay in the late nineteenth century, when a large signal atop Telegraph Hill (then called Signal Hill) announced arriving ships with semaphore. An oft-repeated San Francisco legend has it that one night at the theater an unsuspecting actor called out the rhetorical line, "What does this mean?" while throwing his arms out in a semaphorelike attitude. "Sidewheel steamer," the audience is supposed to have replied as one.

Moving right along, you'll soon arrive at yet another bike path. Make a left onto it from Airport Boulevard and take it ½ mile until it lets out just past the gatehouse at Coyote Point.

Coyote Point once featured an amusement park with beach areas and carnival amusements, but it lasted only a few years before flopping. At present, this wooded promontory features bicycle and walking paths, a golf course, a firing range, beaches, and several extensive picnic grounds. The path through Coyote Point is a little hard to follow in places, but the forested paths are a nice break from the open bayfront of the rest of the route. Following the path becomes easier after you exit the little park.

Once you leave Coyote Point you'll have 9 glorious miles of virtually uninterrupted bayside bike path, all completely flat. The air is rich with the oxygen and swamp gases of marsh lowlands—that, and landfill off-gases. The wind can be stiff. The path may be a little crowded around lunchtime and before and after work but is typically much less crowded than, say, the Sawyer Camp Trail.

The path runs along a levee built in the early 1960s by Texas oil magnate Jack Foster. Prior to Foster's development, what is now Foster City was a giant wetlands surrounding Brewer Island. The first assault on the swamps came when the Leslie and Schilling salt companies set up camp on Brewer Island and began creating salt-evaporation ponds. Then, finally, in 1959, Foster bought the island, built the levee, and drained the wetlands altogether, leaving in their place a series of artificial canals and rows of 1960s-style developments.

Considering the air-scrubbing properties of wetlands and the present unfortunate state of air quality in the Silicon Valley, Foster's alteration may look in hindsight like pretty much of an environmental disaster. Of course, most of the rest of the bay remains lined with wetlands of one sort or another. And, without the levee, there would be no space for Foster City's 28,000 residents and many high-tech office buildings.

The land adjacent to the path doesn't offer much in the way of vegetation. Signs warn trail users to stick to the path. It is kind of chilling to think about an entire aquatic ecosystem buried to make room for the mauve and beige rows of cheap office space and condominiums.

On the bright side, it is flat, so the riding's easy, unless it's windy. And it smells pretty good. Usually. And there's no traffic.

After 9 miles on the Bay Trail, you'll come to a car gate, where the path exits onto a cul-de-sac before picking up on the other side. You'll then pass through a series of fitness stations, where you may want to stop to do some pull-ups, leg raises, or what have you. Just past the fitness stations, the path dumps you on Concourse Drive.

The Foster City bike path continues right on Clipper Drive, but our route stays straight on Concourse another block before turning left onto Island Parkway. Island crosses a small gorge, curves around toward the big office buildings of computer-database giant Oracle, and eventually intersects busy Marine Parkway. Turn right here. Take Marine over the freeway, *taking care* as you merge left four times across freeway on- and off-ramps. Marine then becomes Ralston Avenue. After that, it's 2 blocks farther to El Camino Real. One block to the right on El Camino Real you'll find the Belmont CalTrain station, where you can catch a train back to Millbrae or all the way back to San Francisco.

Trains run quite frequently. You can call CalTrans for scheduling information; the number is (800) 660–4287. Should you find that you have some time to kill awaiting the train, I'd suggest doing some thrifting at the Salvation Army 2 blocks north on Camino Real. Or you might prefer to ride a few blocks west on Ralston and view the grounds of the College and Convent of the Sisters of Notre Dame. This rambling, French-looking facility was built by William Ralston, the risk-taking financial genius who ran the Bank of California in San Francisco until August 27, 1876, when his body was found floating in San Francisco Bay. The hardy Ralston made a daily habit of bay swimming, and his family contested that the drowning was accidental, but it was probably no coincidence that the previous day investors had made a run on Ralston's failing bank, forcing him to close the doors.

If you prefer to ride back to San Francisco via an alternative route, you can take Ralston all the way up to Skyline Boulevard, where you can turn right and pick up the route for The Freeway South (Ride 24). You'll have to ride it in reverse, of course. And, as the name "Skyline" might suggest, it ain't flat.

Central Peaks

Number of miles:	10.1
Approximate pedaling time:	1 hour
Terrain:	Hilly and steep
Traffic:	Light except one stretch of Market, which you can walk
Things to see:	Cole Valley, UC Medical Center, Sutro Tower up close and personal, Twin Peaks reservoirs, Christmas Tree Point overlook, Marietta Street overlook, Mt. Davidson, Easter Cross, Upper Market overpass, Pemberton Stairs, Tank Hill

Of all the rides in this book, I guess this one's my favorite. It's the one I take out-of-town friends on. If they don't ride bikes, we walk it, adding in staircases and forest paths. A tired guest is a good guest, I always say.

The central hills of the city offer the loftiest perspective on the city, and unlike some of the more famous San Francisco hills, they offer lots of natural beauty along with the urban views. There are amazing parklands and overlooks here, if you know how to find them. This ride will give you the basics, although frankly I've kept back the truly special spots. You'll just have to explore on your own.

Begin at the Tassajara Bakery, on Parnassus Avenue at Cole Street. This historic bakery was once run by the Zen center of the same name. I used to work there, then. There were signs taped to the cash register reminding us to breathe. BREATHE, they said. It was good advice considering we sometimes averaged four customers per minute.

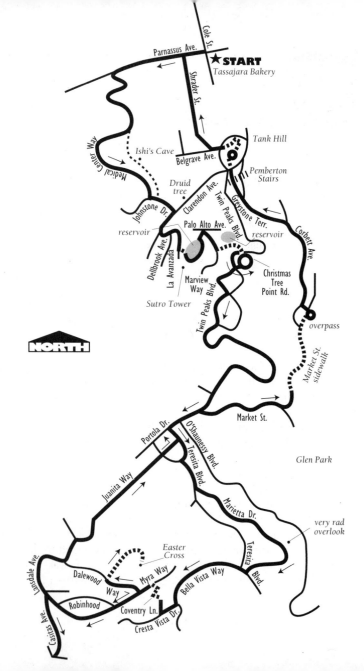

Cole St.

Parnassus Ave.

★ **START**
Tassajara Bakery

Shrader St.

Tank Hill

Ishi's Cave

Medical Center Way

Belgrave Ave.

Pemberton Stairs

Druid tree

Johnstone Dr.

Clarendon Ave.

Twin Peaks Blvd.

Greystone Terr.

reservoir

Corbett Ave.

Palo Alto Ave.

reservoir

Dellbrook Ave.

La Avanzada

Marview Way

Christmas Tree Point Rd.

Sutro Tower

Twin Peaks Blvd.

overpass

NORTH

Market St. sidewalk

Market St.

Portola Dr.

O'Shaunnessy Blvd.

Teresita Blvd.

Glen Park

Juanita Way

Teresita Blvd.

Marietta Dr.

very rad overlook

Teresita Blvd.

Easter Cross

Lansdale Ave.

Dalewood Way

Myra Way

Bella Vista Way

Robinhood Way

Coventry Ln.

Casitas Ave.

Cresta Vista Dr.

0.0	From the Tassajara Bakery, Parnassus at Cole, start west on Parnassus.
0.3	Turn left onto Medical Center Way.
1.1	Turn left onto Johnstone Drive.
1.2	Turn right onto Clarendon Avenue.
1.3	Turn left onto Dellbrook Avenue.
1.4	Turn left onto La Avanzada.
1.6	Turn left, continue around reservoir.
1.7	Turn right onto path to Palo Alto and Marview Way. Turn right onto Marview Way.
1.8	Turn left onto dirt path past reservoir.
1.9	Turn right onto Twin Peaks Boulevard.
2.1	Turn left onto Christmas Tree Point Road.
2.3	Turn left onto Twin Peaks Boulevard.
3.4	Turn right onto Portola Drive.
3.5	Turn left onto O'Shaunessy Boulevard, then make immediate right into parking lot.
3.6	Turn left onto Teresita Boulevard.
3.8	Turn left on Marietta Drive.
4.5	Stop at overlook.
4.6	Turn right onto Teresita, then make immediate left onto Bella Vista Way.
5.0	Turn right onto Cresta Vista Drive.
5.1	Turn right onto Coventry Court. Continue on Coventry Lane.
5.2	Turn left onto Myra Way, then stay right on Dalewood Way past bus stop and trailhead.
5.3	Turn right at second trailhead.
5.6	Turn around at top of Mt. Davidson.
5.9	Turn left onto Dalewood.
6.0	Turn right onto Lansdale Avenue.
6.3	Turn left onto Casitas Avenue.
6.6	Turnaround.
6.9	Turn left onto Lansdale Avenue.
7.0	Turn right onto Juanita Way.
7.6	Turn left onto Teresita Boulevard.

7.7	Turn right onto Portola Drive. Portola becomes Market Street.
8.5	Turn right onto spiral overpass.
8.6	Turn right onto Corbett Avenue.
8.9	Turn left onto Greystone Terrace.
9.2	Turn left onto Clarendon Avenue.
9.3	Turn right up stairs to Tank Hill.
9.4	Head down dirt stairs to Belgrave Avenue.
9.5	Take slanting right onto Shrader Street.
10.0	Turn right onto Parnassus Avenue.
10.1	End at Tassajara Bakery at Cole Street.

Things have slowed a little since the coffeehouse boom, but the Tassajara is still a good meeting place and high-octane fuel stop. The ride ahead, though not long, is arduous.

When you're ready to go, roll up Parnassus toward UC Medical Center. It's a gradual climb of 4 blocks.

When you crest the hill at the medical center, make an immediate left onto Medical Center Way. Notice the sign here that proclaims it as private property and advises that the right to pass is subject to the approval of the owner. I think that translates to, "Be quiet through here! It's a hospital! There are medical students in the dorms here who have been on call for the last forty-eight hours and want to get some sleep. Be courteous!"

The road is narrow and forested, a wonderful four- to ten-minute climb. Near the bottom you can often hear mournful, hangdog barks from canine death row, the kennels of medical science. At the top you arrive at the married-student housing. Here you should be especially quiet and considerate.

Medical Center Way ends on Johnstone Drive. Our route goes left. If you have time, though, you may want to explore to the right, which takes you up to the top of Mt. Sutro, where lots of trees prevent great views. There are nice open meadows, though, making for a very natural setting.

After turning left onto Johnstone, you'll soon pass the chancellor's quarters, on the left. There is a small parking lot here just off Johnstone, and at the end of it a trail begins that leads down to the UC campus through a forest where Ishi once lived.

Ishi, the last member of a tribe near Mt. Lasssen, was found wandering near Oroville and taken to UCSF in 1911. There, he lived and taught anthropologists his language. Later, he lived out his days in a small cave in Sutro Forest before dying of tuberculosis. Ishi's story is recorded in *Ishi of Two Worlds*, by Theodora Kroeber.

Past the chancellor's house, continue down a short, steep hill with swollen speed bumps to Clarendon Avenue, a busy street where we turn right.

Cross over Clarendon and get in the left-turn lane. *Be wary* of oncoming traffic, which can pop quickly over the hill, as you make a left turn onto Dellbrook Avenue. Then, make the next left, onto La Avanzada.

La Avanzada climbs up to the reservoir at the foot of mighty Sutro Tower. When you get to the guardhouse, turn left past some anticar posts and circle around the reservoir. The paved jogging path is $\frac{1}{5}$ mile around. Looming overhead, 980-foot Sutro Television Tower, tallest structure in San Francisco, raises its three mighty trestles like an immense, freestanding, iron empire-waist dress. It was built in 1973 by a group of TV stations. There are lots of fog lights on Sutro Tower, and they flash from bottom to top when the humidity is rising and from top to bottom when the barometer is falling. Ride a couple of times around the reservoir; then find and take the exit onto Palo Alto Avenue.

Go right onto Palo Alto, and then right onto Marview Way. After 1 block, look for a dirt path on the left and turn onto it. It leads past another, uncovered reservoir. This is one of several high-elevation reservoirs installed after the great quake and fire of 1906. Huge 8-inch cast-iron mains connect them with hydrants around the city in a system completely separate from the drinking water supply.

The path gets a little steep at the top, and there's some poison oak along the right edge. It ends on Twin Peaks Boulevard. Hop the guardrail and make a right, up the hill. From here it's just a short way to the top, where you can make a left and ride around Christmas Tree Point Road.

The city lights of San Francisco do resemble a twinkling Christmas Tree, but this short, circular drive was named for the huge Christmas tree the city put up annually during the 1920s.

There are always lots of tourists here. Hang out and see how many languages you can recognize. Market Street points right at Twin Peaks, so looking out over the city it stands out. At night the Path of Gold historic street lighting along its length rolls out toward the bay.

After completing the loop on Christmas Tree Drive, ride back to Twin Peaks Boulevard. If you're getting tired and want to head back, turn right. Ride down Twin Peaks Boulevard, cross over Clarendon, and pick up the route where it climbs the wooden stairs up to Tank Hill.

If you're up for continuing on to Mt. Davidson, at 927 feet the highest peak in town, turn left onto Twin Peaks Boulevard, which is one-way and braids around the Twin Peaks. The south and north summits of Twin Peaks are the second and fourth highest in town, at 922 and 904 feet, respectively (third highest is Mt. Sutro, at 908 feet). Spanish settlers knew Twin Peaks as *Pechos de la Choca,* or Squaw Breasts, a translation of the indigenous name.

When Twin Peaks Boulevard ends on Market, turn right. Market Street changes to Portola Drive here. Move immediately into the left lane. Wait for the left-turn light and begin turning onto O'Shaunessy Boulevard. Instead of continuing, however, stop at the Miraloma Strip Mall on the right. You can't ride past it on the one-way street through the parking lot, so dismount and walk your bike on the sidewalk a short way, toward the Tower Market. Just before it, make a left onto Teresita Boulevard.

Follow Teresita until you see Marietta Drive, and make a left. Continue on Marietta until it splits into one-way streets. Then, all of a sudden, it will break out of the houses and into an open view of Glen Park past an outcropping of folded rock striations.

The best views are not always from the highest places. This is one of my favorite places in the city. Stop for a rest here. Walk out to the rocks. You can hear birds singing. The wide-angle view encompasses City College, Mt. San Bruno, the small blue tower atop McLaren Park, the 280 corridor, and Glen Park, the tiny neighborhood that

O'Shaunessy winds down to below. O'Shaunessy is the longest uninterrupted surface road in the city and is a great bicycle descent when traffic is light.

When ready, continue on Marietta. At Teresita, turn right. Then, 5 yards later, make an immediate left, onto Bella Vista Way, and begin the haul up Mt. Davidson.

At Cresta Vista Drive, turn right. Then, a block later, look for Coventry Court on the right. Turn into it despite the NOT A THROUGH STREET sign.

If you like unusual houses, continue on Cresta Vista a little bit past Coventry and check out number 297. At night a light in the tank atop the stairs illuminates giant aquarium goldfish inside this terrarium for humans.

At the top of Coventry, a small lane continues, zigzagging steeply up.

At Myra Way turn left and edge around Mt. Davidson Park. Bypass the first trailhead, near the bus stop, and continue onto Dalewood Way to another, better trailhead a little farther up. This trail is smooth and rideable on road bikes with low gears.

Up top, leviathan views await, unless it's foggy and dripping. There's also a big chunk of cement called the Easter Cross. At sunrise on Easter, mass is held beneath this monstrous 140-foot cruciform monolith. The landmark cross is being swallowed by tree growth, which some people actually find regrettable.

Return on the same path. Make a left onto Dalewood Way unless pressed for time, in which case turn right and then right again onto Lansdale Avenue to rejoin the main route.

After turning left on Dalewood, turn right on Lansdale at the next intersection.

When you get to Casitas Avenue, turn left. *Casitas* means "little houses" in Spanish. I think you will agree there are some nice little houses on Casitas.

At the bottom of Casitas, turn around and climb back up. Make a left onto Lansdale, which drops steeply into a tight right turn, then drops into a saddle.

You need to make a left at the bottom of the saddle to stay on

Lansdale, but rather than use up your brakes, it's fun to carry your momentum up the other side, turn around, coast up the other side, and so on until you are going slow enough to turn without braking. If you're really good, you can do roll-back turnarounds, Dukes of Hazzard–style.

Pretty soon you'll come to an intersection with Juanita Way to the right and Marne Avenue to the left. Marne leads to an excellent overpass over Portola Drive. Take it if you want to explore Forest Hills. Otherwise, follow the main Central Peaks route by turning right onto Juanita.

Watch between houses on the left for an incredible octagonal eagle's-nest house, atop the cliff across the way. Whew! Must be something, living up there. (You can get to this and other amazing houses by taking the aforementioned overpass, going straight on Kensington Way, and then right at every opportunity, onto Vasquez Avenue, Garcia Avenue, and Edgehill Way.)

Juanita takes us back to Teresita. Go left there, and then right onto busy Portola Drive. You have to ride on Portola for a few blocks. It is a large, intimidating street, and within a block, the right lane turns into Diamond Heights Boulevard, forcing you to merge left. If traffic is bad, or at night, you may want to take the sidewalk. Portola soon changes its name to Market Street.

Continue down Market Street. The view is spectacular. After the scenic lookout, there is an immense sidewalk on the right. Lift your bike up onto it and ride down, appreciating the view without worrying about cars.

When you come to a spiral-ramped pedestrian overpass, ride up and over Market Street. Put in your lowest gear for the steep grunt on the other side up to Corbett Street, where you take a right.

Continue on Corbett to Greystone Terrace. Go left there. Soon Villa Terrace splits off to the right. Stay left on Greystone. It becomes one-way, so continue by walking your bike along the right sidewalk of this virtually traffic-free back street.

Watch for the Pemberton Stairs, which bisect Greystone. Stop there and check out the view, between two buildings, of downtown. These stairs go from Clayton all the way up to Crown Terrace, a very nice walk, especially when combined with the nearby Vulcan and Saturn stairs.

Continue on Greystone until it comes out on Clarendon Avenue. Across the street and a little to the left, look for a small set of wooden stairs. Shoulder your bike and climb the steps. At the top continue along the path into Tank Hill.

A large, circular cement slab remains from the days when a large water tank occupied this spot. Past the slab, the path continues to a rock outcropping overlooking Cole Valley and much of the city, from Golden Gate Park to downtown. Once again, the best views aren't always from the highest places.

Past the rocks, the path continues down to Belgrave Avenue. Some recently built steps make this dirt path a little more difficult to ride down than it used to be.

At Belgrave continue down to an angling right onto Shrader Street. Shrader Street takes you to Parnassus, where you can make a right and, in 1 block, arrive back at the Tassajara Bakery starting point.

There you have it, a quick tour of a few of the central peaks. In addition to these, there are Mt. Olympus (the geographic center of the city), Buena Vista, Corona Heights, and, on the other side of Twin Peaks, Edge Hill, Forest Hills (the top of Mendoza Avenue), Sunset Heights (where you can hike to a spot where the beacons atop the towers of the Golden Gate Bridge align exactly—the towers are 746 feet above sea level, but, accounting for the curvature of the earth, the hill is higher), and Grandview Park. I'll leave you to explore them on your own.

SFO Ramble

Number of miles:	16.1
Approximate pedaling time:	90 minutes
Terrain:	Flat to rolling
Traffic:	Moderate
Things to see:	Jack Kerouac railyard, an early Strauss drawbridge, Mission Rock Terminal, Hunter's Point shipyards, Candlestick Hill, Brisbane, San Bruno Mountain, Oyster Point, SFO north terminal gallery space

If you plan on bringing your bike on an airline flight, you can help offset the outrageous fees charged to take bicycles on domestic routes by riding yourself out to the airport, thereby saving the $15 or so the shuttle buses charge. Just call ahead to make sure your airline can sell you one of those giant cardboard bike boxes, usually for $3.00, and arrive early enough to take off the pedals and turn the handlebars sideways.

If you're running behind schedule, this ride can be done in about forty-five minutes one-way, but it's better to plan on an hour, or even an hour and a half if, like me, you like as little stress as possible, and perhaps a few scenic detours, when traveling.

This ride can also make a pleasant urban excursion, especially in times of light traffic. For most downtown workers it makes a reasonable, if hardly pastoral, lunchtime escape. It goes past McLaren Park, the best place for strenuous lunchtime riding. You could use this route to get to an event at 3 Com Park or to visit San Bruno, Millbrae, or Burlingame. It also links up with the Foster City Flats route (Ride 13), the flattest and most traffic-free in this book.

Begin at Market and Second streets, near the Montgomery BART

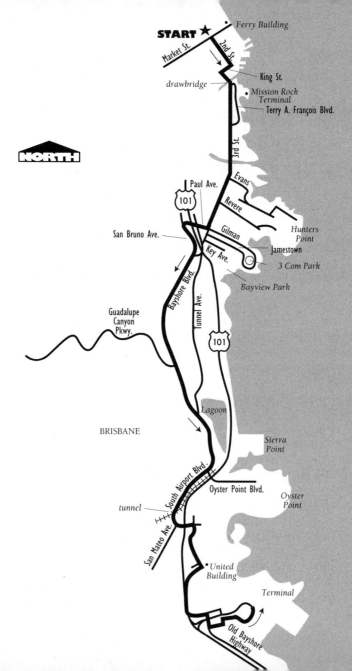

START

Ferry Building

Market St.

2nd St.

King St.

drawbridge

Mission Rock
Terminal

Terry A. François Blvd.

3rd St.

Evans

Paul Ave.

101

Revere

San Bruno Ave.

*Hunters
Point*

Gilman

Key Ave.

Jamestown

3 Com Park

Bayview Park

NORTH

Bayshore Blvd.

Tunnel Ave.

101

Guadalupe
Canyon
Pkwy.

Lagoon

BRISBANE

*Sierra
Point*

South Airport Blvd.

Oyster Point Blvd.

*Oyster
Point*

tunnel

San Mateo Ave.

•*United
Building*

Terminal

Old Bayshore
Highway

DIREC-TIONS at a glance

0.0   Start at Market and Second streets.
0.8   Second Street ends; turn right onto King Street.
1.0   Turn left onto Third Street.
5.2   Turn right onto Paul Avenue.
5.6   Turn left onto San Bruno Avenue.
6.6   Turn right onto Bayshore Boulevard.
11.5   Continue through tunnel.
11.6   Turn left onto San Mateo, under freeway.
11.7   Turn right onto South Airport Boulevard.
13.0   Turn right onto Old Bayshore Highway.
15.6   Turn right, following signs to terminal.
15.9   Turn left, following signs to terminal.
16.1   Turn left, following signs to terminal.

station. Head south on Second. At ⁸⁄₁₀ mile turn right on King Street and ride toward a railroad yard where Jack Kerouac once worked. At Third Street make a left and ride toward a drawbridge that crosses Mission Street.

This bascule drawbridge with concrete counterbalance is of the type Joseph Strauss, chief engineer of the Golden Gate bridge, developed and marketed in starting his own engineering firm in Chicago. Prior to the Strauss design, massive pig-iron ingots were used as weights, which, though smaller in volume than concrete, often accounted for half the cost of a bridge. Strauss kept offices in the Palace Hotel before the Golden Gate project began and probably built this very bridge.

Continue south on Third Street, toward the industrial underbelly of San Francisco, with its interesting smells and sounds. If you feel like escaping traffic, turn left immediately after crossing the bridge, ride down to the water, and turn right onto Terry A. François Boulevard. This route takes you past the Mission Rock Terminal, where fishermen will sometimes sell you shrimp on the cheap early in the morning, and past waterfront bar/grills like The Ramp and Olive Oyls, where on sunny afternoons you can lounge out on the pier and take in live music. Eventually François turns into Mariposa Street and takes you back to Third Street.

After you pass Cesar Chavez Street, the cross streets become alphabetical and you enter the ethnic, working-class Bayview district. It's a low-income area, and there are often desperate characters milling about—it's a good idea to *keep alert*, but this is also an interesting area to explore.

You can take Evans Avenue to Hunters Point Boulevard, which runs out to a former shipbuilding and repair center, now a naval installation. Without a pass you won't be allowed to continue on to the former shipbuilding structures, many of which now house artist's studios. Open Studios are held twice a year, however. Call (415) 861–9838 for information.

A bit farther south on Third Street you'll start to climb a little over the shoulder of Candlestick Hill, and you'll see freeway entrance signs over the roadway. If you feel like taking a side trip to a truly spectacular hilltop park, make a left onto Key Avenue, just before the freeway signs. At the top of Key, continue past a car gate up a sharply steepening paved path leading up to Bayview Park, a very dramatic picnic spot overlooking the 101 levee and South San Francisco.

If you just want to get to the airport, from Third Street turn right onto Paul Avenue, which comes 3 blocks before Key Avenue and is easy to miss because it is called Gilman Avenue to the left and heavily signed as such. Gilman Avenue goes to 3 Com Park, as does Jamestown just ahead. Jamestown Avenue is the more direct route choice.

On Paul you'll climb for ½ mile, cross Bayshore Boulevard, then pass under Highway 101. Take the first left onto San Bruno Avenue and continue climbing next to the freeway. Soon you'll level out, curve downhill to the right, and arrive on Bayshore, where you have a choice.

If you like really quiet roads, make a left onto Bayshore, an immediate right onto Blanken Avenue, and the first right onto Tunnel Road. Tunnel is a little bit of tranquillity in a storm of traffic. It runs

for almost 4 miles before ending on Bayshore.

The other option is to merge right on Bayshore and just follow Bayshore through Brisbane. I usually stay on Bayshore, which has a good shoulder, unless traffic seems unusually bad.

Bayshore is home to several Tijuana-style statuary yards, industrial-supply companies, and San Francisco's main landfill in Guadalupe Canyon. Soon you'll pass Guadalupe Canyon Parkway, which climbs up to San Bruno Mountain. A little bit farther you'll see a lagoon and a nice residential neighborhood on the right.

Past Brisbane you'll pass Oyster Point Boulevard, which you can take left to a marina popular with windsurfers. Past Oyster Point you enter South San Francisco, and Bayshore changes its name to Airport Boulevard. One mile farther you'll pass through a tunnel and come to an intersection with San Mateo Avenue. Turn left here and pass under Highway 101. Make the next right onto South Airport Boulevard.

Take South Airport until it dead-ends just past a huge United Airlines building and turn right onto Old Bayshore Highway. Old Bayshore changes its name to McDonnel Road and curves left under the shoulder of an elevated freeway for a little more than a mile before curving gently left into the airport. At this point follow signs to the terminal, making a right, a quick left after the underpass, and another left before merging with traffic heading for the terminal.

If meeting someone on the lower arrival level, you'll need to cross over a few lanes of freeway speed traffic. It may be safer to stay right, ride up to the departure level, and find some stairs to take down to the lower level.

If you're meeting some folks without too much luggage, take them up to the upper departure level and all the way around the semicircular Terminal Way to the far end of the north terminal. Put them on the SamTrans 7F—at $2.50 a cheap alternative to the shuttle buses—and race them back to the city. They'll win unless an event at 3 Com Park has just finished.

The north terminal and the walkway between it and the main terminal house excellent museum spaces that often host free shows of international quality. For information on current shows call the Arts Commissions Bureau of Exhibits at (415) 876–2416.

For the return trip continue out past the terminal and make a right just before a Chevron gas station. This short road takes you to McDonnel, where you can take a left and retrace the route back to the city.

Port Costa Loop

Number of miles:	34.4
Approximate pedaling time:	3 hours
Terrain:	Flat to rolling
Traffic:	Very light on weekends
Things to see:	Iron Horse Bike Trail, Contra Costa Canal Trail, Shell Oil Museum, Martinez, Carquinez Straits, Port Costa Materials, Inc. (brick factory), Port Costa, The Warehouse Bar

This mellow, mosey-along kind of ride offers highly scenic views of Mt. Diablo and the East Bay Hills as well as of the Carquinez Straits and the tiny and ancient hamlet of Port Costa. I don't know which is the bigger treat: riding the eroded and unrepaired Carquinez Scenic Road, which is closed to cars, or shooting the bull with the locals at The Warehouse, an immense, historic bar in Port Costa right out of a country-music video. Then, of course, there's the John Muir House to be visited, charming downtown Martinez to peruse, and the uncrowded multiuse paths of Contra Costa County to check out.

If you don't know about these bike paths, there are more than 100 miles of them, most rails-to-trails conversions. They aren't as crowded as paths in more urban areas. Since they run for miles and miles, interrupted only by the occasional cross street, you can travel significant distances on them with nary a thought to traffic or navigation. They are a good way for people from elsewhere to see a sampling of the county without needing to become familiar with specific streets. For free maps or to report messes or make complaints, call (510) 635–0138.

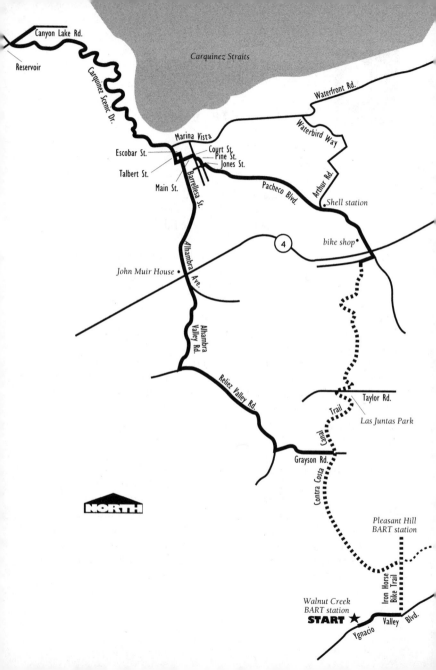

**DIREC-
TIONS
at a glance**

0.0   Start at Walnut Creek BART station. Go left onto Ygnacio Valley Boulevard.

0.4   Turn left onto Iron Horse Bike Trail.

1.6   Turn left onto Contra Costa Canal Trail.

2.6   Avoid right onto another bike path.

5.1   Las Juntas Park.

5.7   Bad intersection with Taylor Road.

8.2   Path ends; turn right onto John Muir Road.

8.5   Turn left onto Pacheco Boulevard.

9.9   Turn left at Shell station to stay on Pacheco.

12.3   Turn left onto Jones Street.

12.4   Turn right onto Pine Street.

12.5   Turn left onto Mellus Street, which becomes Court Street.

12.6   Turn left onto Main Street.

13.0   Turn right onto Talbert Street.

15.4   Continue past barricades into Shoreline Park.

18.3   Turn right onto Reservoir.

18.6   Turn right onto Canyon Lake Road.

18.9   The Warehouse bar on the right

19.5   Turn left onto Carquinez Scenic Drive.

22.4   Continue past barricades out of Shoreline Park.

24.6   Turn left onto Escobar Street.

24.7   Turn right onto Barrellesa Street.

26.5   John Muir House.

27.1   Turn right onto Alhambra Valley Road.

28.4   Turn left onto Reliez Valley Road.

30.6   Turn left onto Grayson Road.

31.6   Turn right onto Contra Costa Canal Trail.

34.0   Turn left onto Iron Horse Bike Trail.

34.4   End at Pleasant Hill BART.

The ride starts from the Walnut Creek BART and ends up at the Pleasant Hill station. Round-trip fare from San Francisco, at present, is just over $5.00. If you don't care to see downtown Walnut Creek, you might prefer to start and finish at Pleasant Hill. It should be pretty clear from the map how to do this.

The Walnut Creek BART station has an elevated platform, and after detraining there you might wish to take advantage of the excellent view to get your bearings. To the west you will see trees and some hills and Highway 680. To the east looms Mt. Diablo. Leading toward Mt. Diablo is a huge six-lane menace, Ygnacio Valley Boulevard. Our route takes Ygnacio through downtown Walnut Creek for 3 blocks before picking up the Iron Horse Bike Trail.

Because Ygnacio is so busy, it is legal to ride on the sidewalk here. Since we'll take the Iron Horse Trail to the left off Ygnacio, it is probably easiest to ride or walk on the near sidewalk as you go left from the station on Ygnacio. Soon, you'll pass the California Bike and Snowboard shop, a handy last-minute tube or Powerbar stop.

Once the trail starts, turn left. After $1\frac{7}{10}$ miles you'll come to an intersection with another bike path. Straight ahead lies the Pleasant Hill BART station, but for now go left onto the Contra Costa Canal Trail, which you'll stay on for the next 7 miles or so.

When you find yourself climbing a short hill into Las Juntas Park, you may wish to take a rest stop and get a drink of water. This small park has excellent views.

Just past there the path crosses busy Taylor Road, and it is necessary to ride left all the way to a signaled crosswalk, cross, and pick up the Canal Trail again. This involves making a left after a 270-degree turn.

Continue on the Contra Costa Canal Trail until you get to John Muir Road, which parallels Highway 4, an elevated freeway also called the John Muir Parkway. Turn right on Muir Road. After the freeway on-ramp on the left, get in the left lane and take a left onto Pacheco Boulevard.

Pacheco can be busy on weekdays, with lots of commuter traffic. It has a decent shoulder, but the fog line is vague and there is often lots of debris and glass on the shoulder. Not the prettiest part of the ride.

Just after crossing under the freeway, look for Martinez Cyclery on the left, where the legendary Chuck Tyler of the Cyclery Group works. This classic shop has a devoted clientele.

A mile and a half later, in order to stay on Pacheco, it is necessary to make a left at a Shell Oil station.

Past there, on the right, look for the Shell Oil Planter Box, a concrete scallop shell with flowers growing through it. A short way later, on Arreba Street in Martinez, a sign points right to the Shell Oil Alumni Museum.

Next thing you know, you're in downtown Martinez, a small town with many beautiful old buildings. Make a left onto Jones Street, then a right onto Pine Street, which turns into Court Street. Then, go left onto Main Street. Dimaggio's Coffee Shop, on the right in a few blocks, is owned by a cyclist who will let you bring your bike inside.

Continue on Main to Talbart Street and turn right. After 3 blocks continue onto Carquinez Scenic Drive. You'll find yourself climbing through a beautiful and very Spanish-looking old graveyard (unfortunately, it's closed to visitors), the Catherine de Siena Cemetery. A short way past there, the road closes to cars and continues on past several dramatic slides, with postcard views of the Carquinez Straits.

Forty percent of the land area of California drains its runoff water through these straits. The Sacramento River, which drains the Southern Cascades (Mt. Shasta and Mt. Lassen), and the San Joaquin, which drains the mighty Sierras, highest mountains in the continental United States, flow together near Pittsburg before continuing on through these straits, which lead into San Francisco Bay and then through the Golden Gate, the only break in a 400-mile wall of coastal mountains.

Much of the Sacramento's water is now diverted by huge pumps near Tracy for agricultural purposes and to Los Angeles. You might have seen the aqueduct, which Highway 80 crosses. The pumps suck up baby fish. The virtual extinction of winter-spawning salmon has been blamed on reduced freshwater flow into the San Francisco Bay.

After a few miles of quiet and scenic road, you'll arrive at Port Costa Materials, Inc., a large brick factory with rail and aquatic transfer capabilities. Past the factory, the road carries car traffic again.

From there it's just a few miles into the tiny, tiny town of Port Costa. Be on the lookout for a sharp right onto Reservoir Street and drop on down to a place that looks more like a Nevada ghost town than a typical Bay Area suburb. Down in town, turn right onto Canyon Lake Road.

At the end of town, you'll find the imposing earth building of The Warehouse, with bar, restaurant, pool table, antiques shop, and a menu of more than 250 beers. Have yourself a Belgian Lambic and kick back out on the patio for a while. Or tell a few tall tales to the crowd inside. Tell them you are an old friend of Juanita, the immense and spirited cook of many years there immortalized in *Juanita's Eat It or Wear It* cookbook, by Sally Hayton-Keeva.

When it's time to return, retrace the route back to Martinez. There, make a right onto Talbart Street, a left on Escobar Street, and a right onto Berrellesa Street.

Berrellesa soon turns into Alhambra Avenue, passing by the John Muir Historic Site, where the great naturalist and poet ran a fruit farm and wrote. There are hiking trails and guided tours and a ranger station with lots of books and souvenirs.

Nearby there's even a strip mall named for the father of our National Park System. What do you suppose he would think of that?

A little past the Muir House, make a right onto Alhambra Valley Road, as Alhambra Avenue continues left.

Next, make a right onto Reliez Valley Road. Take this pleasantly rolling road to Grayson Road, where you can make a left, ride a short way, and turn right back onto the Canal Trail.

Continue south on the Canal Trail until it intersects the Iron Horse Trail. This time, take a left and continue onto the Pleasant Hill BART.

There you have it, the Port Costa Loop. If you enjoyed it, call Carolyn Helmke at RIDES for Bay Area Commuters and thank her directly: (415) 861–7665.

Two Sides of Town

Number of miles:	28.3
Approximate pedaling time:	3 hours
Terrain:	First half hilly, second half flat
Traffic:	First half light, second half heavy
Things to see:	Laguna Honda, Forest Hills, Marietta overlook, Glen Park, City College, Mission Terrace, McLaren Park, Portola District, Third Street, South of Market, Zeitgeist Bar, SF Mint, Antique Trolley Cars, Lower Haight, Haight Ashbury

This route cuts crosswise from the northwest to the southeast corner of San Francisco, from the Sunset, up past Forest Hills, past City College, through Mission Terrace to McLaren Park, the Portola District, and points beyond along the eastern edge of the peninsula. It then returns through downtown on a popular commuting route from South of Market back to the Sunset. Essentially, it is two crosstown routes put together to make a loop.

If you live in the Sunset, you'll probably use a route similar to the return leg for both going to and coming home from work. But on mornings when you've got a little extra time, why not try this scenic outbound leg? You could also take it if you're headed for points south of Bernal Heights and wish to avoid downtown traffic.

From Ocean Beach, at the extreme western edge of the peninsula, head toward town on Kirkham Street. Kirkham is generally the fastest street to take during heavy-traffic times. High-speed drivers ruin Golden Gate Park during rush hour, and it's really cold in there in the

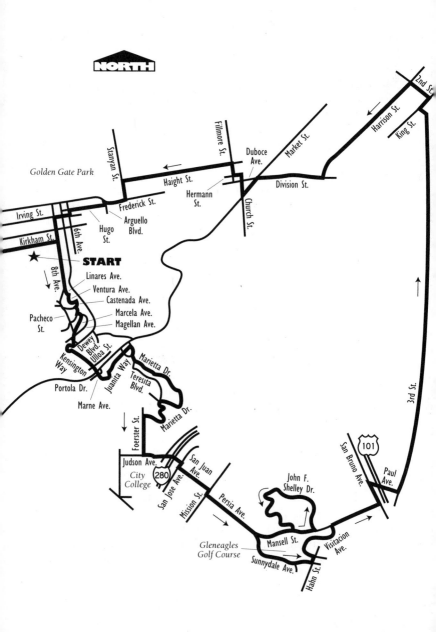

NORTH

Golden Gate Park

Stanyan St.

Fillmore St.

Duboce Ave.

Market St.

2nd St.

Harrison St.

King St.

Haight St.

Hermann St.

Division St.

Irving St.

Frederick St.

Church St.

Kirkham St.

6th Ave.

Hugo St.

Arguello Blvd.

START

8th Ave.

Linares Ave.

Ventura Ave.

Castenada Ave.

Marcela Ave.

Magellan Ave.

Pacheco St.

Dewey Blvd.

Ulloa St.

Marietta Dr.

Kensington Way

Juanita Way

Teresita Blvd.

Portola Dr.

Marne Ave.

Marietta Dr.

Foerster St.

Judson Ave.

City College

280

San Juan Ave.

San Jose Ave.

Mission St.

Persia Ave.

John F. Shelley Dr.

101

San Bruno Ave.

Paul Ave.

3rd St.

Mansell St.

Visitacion Ave.

Gleneagles Golf Course

Sunnydale Ave.

Hahn St.

DIREC-TIONS
at a glance

0.0	From Great Highway head east on Kirkham Street.
3.0	Turn right onto Eighth Avenue.
3.6	Turn left onto Linares Avenue.
3.7	Turn right onto Ventura Avenue.
3.8	Turn right onto Castenada Avenue.
3.9	Turn left onto Magellan Avenue.
4.0	Turn right onto Marcela Avenue.
4.2	Turn left onto Pacheco Street.
4.3	Turn right onto Dewey Boulevard.
4.5	Ride around roundabout; take right onto Kensington Way.
4.9	Take overpass over Portola Drive.
5.0	Continue on Marne Avenue.
5.1	Turn left onto Juanita Way.
5.7	Turn right onto Teresita Boulevard.
5.9	Turn left onto Marietta Drive.
6.5	Turn left onto Teresita Boulevard.
7.0	Turn left onto Foerster Street.
7.4	Turn left onto Judson Avenue.
7.8	Turn right onto San Jose Avenue.
7.9	Turn left onto San Juan Avenue.
8.3	Turn right onto Mission Street.
8.4	Turn left on Persia Avenue.
8.7	Enter McLaren Park. Persia becomes Mansell Street.
9.5	Turn left onto John F. Shelley Drive.
10.7	Turn right onto Mansell Street.
11.2	Turn left onto Sunnydale Avenue.
11.9	Stay left at Santos Street.
12.0	Turn left onto Hahn Street.
12.1	Turn left onto Visitacion Avenue.
12.6	Turn right onto Mansell Street.
13.3	Turn right onto San Bruno Avenue.
13.4	Turn right onto Paul Avenue.
13.8	Turn left onto Third Street.
18.0	Turn right onto King Street.

18.2 Turn left onto Second Street.
18.7 Turn left onto Harrison Street.
20.1 Turn right onto Division Street.
20.7 Turn left onto Market Street.
20.9 Turn right onto Church Street.
21.1 Turn left onto Hermann Street.
21.2 Turn right onto Fillmore Street.
21.3 Turn left onto Haight Street.
22.5 Turn left onto Stanyan Street.
22.7 Turn right onto Frederick Street.
22.9 Turn left onto Arguello Boulevard.
23.0 Turn right onto Hugo Street.
23.6 Turn left onto Sixth Avenue.
24.3 Turn right onto Irving Street.
25.1 Turn left onto Eighth Avenue.
25.2 Turn right onto Kirkham Street.
28.3 End at Great Highway.

---

early mornings. Cars go too fast on Lincoln. Irving is too congested to ride fast on. The lanes are too narrow on Judah, due to the raised trolley median. Kirkham does have a few hills, but is generally easy otherwise.

When you get to Eighth Avenue, turn right and begin climbing up toward the ritzy suburb of Forest Hills.

Lots of people take Seventh Avenue, which turns into Laguna Honda and climbs up to Portola/Market Street. I use this route sometimes in the other direction, but inbound, the route is slightly uphill and the ravine holds in too much bad air to make exertion pleasant during morning rush hour. Also, traffic speeds are high, and although there is a wide cement sidewalk, it is often covered with litter. Again, however, in the downhill direction, from the top of Market Street, Woodside to Laguna Honda/Seventh Avenue is a good route.

Climbing up Eighth, there's one kind of long, steep block, but at least there are nice gardens to look at. After that it gets easier.

Pretty soon you'll need to make a series of turns to snake through the curving streets of opulent Forest Hills with as little climbing as possible. This requires turning left onto Linares Avenue, right onto Ventura Avenue, right onto Castenada Avenue, left onto Magellan Avenue, and right onto Marcela Avenue. Although it sounds complicated, these turns represent the obvious choices, really, and the route is easy to learn.

Marcela then merges into Pacheco Street, which is really the main drag through Forest Hills. From Pacheco turn right onto Dewey Boulevard. At the roundabout ride almost all the way around and continue onto Kensington Way.

Kensington winds past a beautiful little open space on Knockash Hill. An amazing and delightful number of arboreal play objects may be found by persons exploring this obscure jewel of a park. Cross Ulloa Street and continue up onto the pedestrian overpass over Portola Drive. Once across, turn left briefly onto Miraloma Drive, then right onto Marne Avenue, which curves left and becomes Juanita Way.

Juanita climbs up, parallel to Portola, until it intersects Teresita Boulevard. Go right there. Then, a bit later, go left onto Marietta Drive.

Marietta winds around the edge of Glen Canyon and features a beautiful rocky overlook at one point. Walk out on the rocks to best appreciate the panorama over Glen Park.

Soon Marietta ends at Teresita. Go left.

Teresita then ends at Foerster Street. Turn left again. Soon you'll pass Joost Avenue, which was named for the man who built the electric street cars that brought settlement to the Glen Park neighborhood.

Foerster ends at Judson Avenue. Turn left unless headed for City College, in which case turn right then left onto Phelan Avenue.

Judson drops down to Circular Avenue, which parallels the 280 corridor and presents a variety of overpass options across the massive river of cars. If you take Circular all the way to the left, you'll get to Glen Park. Our main route continues straight on Judson, across the freeway. When Judson ends on San Jose Avenue, jog right ½ block before continuing left onto San Juan Avenue.

San Juan runs through the Mission Terraces neighborhood before finishing up at Mission Street. There, we turn right and go a short ½ block before turning left onto Persia Avenue.

Persia runs through the Excelsior District before changing its name to Mansell Avenue and entering John McLaren Park. This large, rambling, hillside park is underused and completely unknown to many San Franciscans.

Climb up into McLaren Park on Mansell. After the crest of the hill, you'll see John F. Shelley Drive to the left. Keep on Mansell for now, however. Soon you'll see Shelley again. Turn left here to begin a wonderful 3½-mile loop, virtually free of traffic but with tough climbs, one tough neighborhood section, and amazing downtown views on clear days. (If you wish to bypass this loop, just continue straight on Mansell and pick up the main route, turning left onto San Bruno.)

On Shelley you'll climb up to a small blue water tower and then begin a steep descent back down Mansell. Go right there and start climbing again. Then, after a fast descent, make a hard left onto Sunnydale Avenue. Sunnydale climbs for a while before dropping into the devastating poverty of the Sunnydale projects. There, make the first left, onto Hahn Street, and then the next left onto Visitacion Avenue.

Keep a sharp eye here. I've heard of at least one bikejacking in McLaren.

Somehow, frivolous recreation, the province of the privileged, seems almost embarrassing in proximity to the abject poverty of Visitacion Valley. That never seems to stop the golfers from playing at nearby Gleneagles International Golf Course. Actually, though, people tend to play for simple love of the game there. Unlike some other courses in town, this municipal course is relatively unexclusive.

Visitacion climbs very steeply. When it arrives on Mansell, turn right unless you're up for another loop, in which case you'll find Shelley a hundred yards to the left.

Mansell stair-steps down to San Bruno Street, main drag of the Portola/University Mound neighborhood. Turn left there.

Paul Avenue, the next right, takes you under the 101 freeway and, in a few blocks, brings you to Third Street, the fastest way back to downtown. Turn left there.

After crossing the Lefty O'Doul drawbridge, make the first right, onto King Street, a left onto Second Street, and, after riding under Interstate 80, a left onto Harrison Street.

From here back to Ocean Beach, the route follows a popular commute route. It has a lot less climbing, but much more traffic, than the first part of the route.

Harrison, a busy one-way, is a main thoroughfare for cars, but if you stay as far to the right as you can, watch out for doors opening, and go fast enough to flow with the traffic, I think riding here is lots easier than trying to deal with Market Street rush-hour chaos.

At Ninth Avenue, there's a tricky place where you need to merge left across a couple of lanes of traffic turning right. This is one of those instances in which it is so useful to be able to look quickly back over your left shoulder while continuing to ride in a straight line. This is something you should practice in a safe place. It will really come in handy. Mirrors just aren't the same.

Continue on Harrison to Division Street, a road that runs underneath the 101 freeway. Go right here.

You'll almost always have to wait at the light on Mission. The stretch after that is narrow. Cars are also coming off the freeway here, many at excessive speeds. There are two strategies to avoid trouble at this intersection. The first is to jump the light and jam through the narrow part before any cars can pass you. If you don't feel like making the effort, the other strategy is to ride up the ramp onto the sidewalk and weave around the freeway columns. *Be careful* of pedestrians and when merging back onto Division Street, which now becomes Duboce Avenue.

Next you should note the Zeitgeist Bar on the near right corner at Valencia. The Zeitgeist is the classic bikie bar in town. The first Critical Mass rides always used to wind up there. Lots of messengers go there after work on Fridays. Or any other time. Why? It's simple, really. Plentiful bicycle parking in the backyard.

Past the Zeitgeist you'll have to climb for a couple of blocks, up to Market Street, where you usually have to wait for the light.

Many cyclists continue straight over Market Street here and ride the wrong way down 1 block of Duboce Avenue. If there are oncoming cars—which is almost never—they hop up on the sidewalk or squeeze. The legal option would be to turn left onto Market, ride 1 block down to Church Street, and turn right there. Continue up to Hermann Street and turn left. Then, in 1 block, turn right onto Fillmore Street.

On Fillmore, continue 2 blocks up to Haight Street and turn left.

Our route continues on Haight Street to Stanyan Street, where it turns left. If you are really sensitive to climbing, though, you may prefer to turn right onto Scott Street and follow the route known as the "wiggle." I'm not totally certain of the route, but it involves a series of turns that allow you to ride into Golden Gate Park without climbing at all.

Stanyan is pretty hectic, but you only have to take it a couple of blocks. The nice, wide sidewalk can look pretty tempting during high-traffic times, but *do be careful* not to run physically into any policefolk as you ride in front of the Haight Ashbury Police Station. They might give you a ticket.

At Frederick Street turn right. Ride past Kezar Stadium, which has a wonderful rubberized running track open to the public. When Frederick ends on Arguello Boulevard, turn left and ride ½ block uphill. Then, turn right onto Hugo Street, a quiet little backstreet.

Make a left onto Sixth Avenue, a block before Hugo ends, because Seventh Street is too scary. Then, zigzag through the Inner Sunset shopping district, making a right onto Irving Street and a left onto Eighth Avenue. In 2 blocks we're back to Kirkham, which can be ridden back out to the start.

There you have it. Two crosstown routes put together to make a loop. One of the routes is wildly popular, ridden with perhaps a few slight variations by hundreds every day, and the other is all but unknown to most San Francisco cyclists. Hope you had fun.

Marin Freeway

Number of miles:	14.7
Approximate pedaling time:	90 minutes
Difficulty:	Moderate
Terrain:	One 400-foot climb
Traffic:	Busy in places
Things to see:	Camino Alto Preserve, cute Marin shop districts, Bayfront Park, Ross's stop-sign alley

I call this ride the Marin Freeway because it is the designated bike route from San Francisco through suburban Marin. What the 101 freeway is to drivers, this route is to cyclists: the fastest way out of the population belt to points north.

Despite being a "freeway" this route passes through six congested urban zones. It features twenty-two turns, twenty-six stop signs, seventeen stoplights, hundreds of crosswalks, two narrow bridges, and many miles of bike path often clogged with swerving skaters, baby carriages, dogs, and oblivious tourists.

Despite all that this route is actually pleasant enough that hundreds and hundreds of people ride it every day. Many commute along it, and most regular San Francisco and Marin cyclists could probably ride it in their sleep if they had to.

Begin at the north end of the Golden Gate Bridge. For all roads preceding Corte Madera, please refer to the map on pages 164–165 (Ride 21). If you have ridden across on the west sidewalk, follow the path left through a gate and parking lot, turn right and climb a short hill, then make a right and coast down to Alexander Avenue, where you can make a left, go through an underpass, and begin descending to Sausalito. If you have ridden across on the east, multiuse side, exit

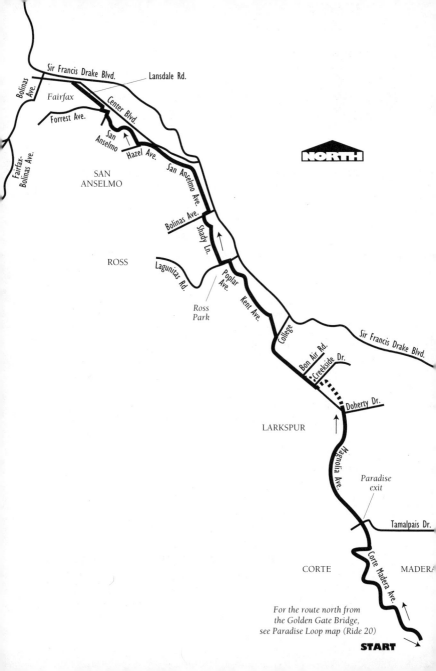

Sir Francis Drake Blvd.

Lansdale Rd.

Bolinas Ave.

Fairfax

Center Blvd.

Forrest Ave.

San Anselmo

Fairfax-Bolinas Ave.

SAN ANSELMO

Hazel Ave.

San Anselmo Ave.

Bolinas Ave.

ROSS

Shady Ln.

Lagunitas Rd.

Poplar Ave.

Kent Ave.

Ross Park

College

Sir Francis Drake Blvd.

Bon Air Rd.

Creekside Dr.

Doherty Dr.

LARKSPUR

Magnolia Ave.

Paradise exit

Tamalpais Dr.

CORTE

Corte Madera Ave.

MADERA

NORTH

For the route north from the Golden Gate Bridge, see Paradise Loop map (Ride 20)

START

DIREC-TIONS at a glance

0.0   (See map on pages 164–165 for the first 6.4 miles.) Start at Golden Gate Bridge, north side. From east sidewalk, follow path through Vista Point and turn right onto Sausalito Lateral/Alexander Avenue. From west sidewalk exit left into parking lot, climb short hill, and turn right onto Conzelman. Turn left onto Sausalito Lateral/Alexander Avenue and proceed through underpass.

1.4   Turn right onto Second Street.

1.5   Turn right onto Richardson Street.

1.6   Turn left onto Bridgeway Boulevard.

3.9   Cross Gate 6 Road; then continue on Richardson Bay bike path.

4.6   Cross Pohono Street.

5.0   Tennessee Valley exit.

5.4   Miller Avenue exit.

6.0   Strawberry-Tiburon exit.

6.3   Turn left on East Blithedale Boulevard.

6.4   Turn right onto Camino Alto. Camino Alto becomes Corte Madera Avenue (see opposite map). Corte Madera becomes Magnolia Avenue.

9.8   Turn right onto bike path after Doherty Drive.

10.0 Exit bike path; continue on Magnolia Avenue.

11.0 Turn left onto Kent Avenue.

11.6 Kent becomes Poplar.

11.9 Turn left onto Lagunitas Road.

12.0 Turn right onto Shady Lane.

12.5 Turn right onto Bolinas Avenue.

12.6 Turn left onto San Anselmo Avenue.

13.1 Turn left onto San Anselmo Avenue, which becomes Hazel Avenue.

13.4 Turn right onto San Anselmo Avenue.

14.1 Turn left onto Lansdale Road.

14.7 End downtown Fairfax.

into the Vista Point parking lot and follow the bike-route signs north out of the parking lot to Sausalito Lateral/Alexander Avenue. Go right onto Alexander and down the hill into Sausalito.

In Sausalito stay on the main drag through town. This requires turning right onto Second Street, right onto Richardson Street, and left onto Bridgeway, but you might not notice these turns since it seems as if you're just following the main drag.

Bridgeway runs along the bay briefly, then through town and finally over two rolling hills before crossing Gate Six Road and turning into a freeway entrance. I usually just stay on Bridgeway all the way through Sausalito, although there is a low-speed designated multiuse path on the right, bay, side that you may prefer if you are extremely sensitive to traffic. Both routes eventually arrive at the intersection of Bridgeway and Gate Six Road, beyond which Bridgeway turns into a freeway entrance. Cross over Gate Six Road here, and continue north on a bike path that starts on the right-hand side of Bridgeway. Thirty yards later you should pass a small path leading right up to Sausalito Cyclery, which has a nice public drinking fountain near its entrance.

Continue on the main bike path—the Richardson Bay bike path—which soon exits onto Pohono Street. Cross this street with care and pick up the path again on the other side. A short distance later, pass beneath the 101 freeway. From there, the path runs on a levee across the floodplain of Richardson Bay and may be surrounded by water during high tide. When that happens you get the eerie but cool sensation of riding your bike on top of the bay!

Please note that this is a multiuse bike path, full of pedestrians, roller skaters, and pregnant women pushing strollers while walking dogs on long leashes. It isn't a time-trial course for cyclists. Marin County offers many good places to go fast, but this isn't one of them.

Shortly after passing under the freeway, you'll come to a wooden bridge. A small path leads off to the left. I call this path the Tennessee Valley exit. The path crosses a floodplain in front of the Dipsea Cafe, an excellent breakfast spot, goes under a bridge, and merges onto Tennessee Valley Road, which winds out to some stables and, after turning to gravel, a cozy beach.

This is also the exit to take if you want the most direct way up Mt.

Tam, although you can expect lots of traffic. Cross the arched wooden bridge, merge into traffic, and the next left puts you on Route 1, the Shoreline Highway, which has signs leading to the top of the mountain. There are definitely more pleasant routes, such as following the Muir Woods Loop route (Ride 21) to Four Corners and making a right onto Panoramic Highway instead of going straight on Muir Woods Road. Or you might ride the Alpine Dam Loop (Ride 22), which is essentially a big loop around Mt. Tam with the option of summiting at one point. Yet another, and probably the easiest route, is to climb the unpaved Old Railroad Grade. Follow the Muir Woods Loop (Ride 21) to the Depot in Mill Valley, and then take Throckmorton up to East Blithedale and turn left. You'll see the gated Old Railroad Grade on the right after a couple of miles.

The Marin Freeway route continues north and soon crosses another wooden bridge. A short way later, a short path exits to the left through some anticar posts onto Miller Avenue. Miller Avenue is the most direct route into downtown Mill Valley, so I call this the Miller, or the Mill Valley exit. Just past it the Marin Freeway route curves to the right and continues.

The next wooden bridge occurs in Bay Front Park, where a path branches off to the right and crosses another, larger wood bridge. This is the Strawberry-Tiburon exit, useful when riding the Paradise Loop (Ride 20) in a counterclockwise direction.

A short while later the path arrives at East Blithedale Avenue, a busy main street of Mill Valley. Our Marin Freeway route turns left here. On the other side of Blithedale, the bike path does continue north, but it is not part of the main route through Marin. Rather, I call it the San Rafael exit. You can follow the route described in China Camp Loop (Ride 23) to ride from here directly to the Larkspur Ferry Terminal, into San Rafael, or, past that, to China Camp or Lucas Valley.

After turning left on East Blithedale, ride 1 block to Camino Alto. There, make a right. Ignore the badly placed NOT A THROUGH STREET sign, which applies to a small road branching off to the right. Begin climbing.

The Camino Alto climb is about 450 feet. The road has a poor shoulder, but traffic is usually light. Keep an ear out for frustrated race-car drivers. At the summit you might want to wait for a car-free interval so that you won't have to keep the brakes clamped all the way down the twisty 400-foot descent.

A three-way stop sign at Tamalpais Drive announces Corte Madera. *Be careful here.* Note that traffic coming up the hill off the freeway doesn't have to stop. You do. When it's clear, proceed through Corte Madera, with its narrow shoulders and parked cars. Unless, of course, you wanted to ride the Paradise Loop clockwise, in which case you'd turn right here onto Tamalpais, also known as the Paradise exit.

Next up is the cute shop district of Larkspur, where Corte Madera Avenue changes into Magnolia Avenue and traffic is usually bumper to bumper. There's a stop sign, then a light; then you cross Doherty Drive and pick up a bike path on the right.

This is a good bike path. It doesn't slow you down too much to take it because there are usually few pedestrians. Soon it empties you back out onto Magnolia, where you cross Creekside and have an opportunity to pick up another bike path on the right. *Don't do it.*

For one thing, Magnolia is plenty wide here. For another, this second bike path segment ends awkwardly, forcing you to enter Magnolia at a blind corner and ride over a pedestrian island. It's dangerous and slow.

Soon you'll come to Bon Air, which can serve as an exit to the Larkspur Ferry and the hilly but traffic-free way over to San Rafael. (The route is described in reverse on the return leg of the China Camp Loop: Go right onto Bon Air, right onto South Eliseo Drive, right onto a bike path, right onto Laderman Way, cross Sir Francis Drake Boulevard, and make a right onto Via La Cumbre.)

Continue another ¾ mile on Magnolia and then, when it curves to the right and turns into College Avenue, take the left lane. After stopping at the sign, make a soft left onto Kent Avenue and continue into the charming town of Ross.

Kent soon changes names to Poplar Avenue and passes Ross Commons Park, where there is always lots of car traffic. *Beware* of diagonal parkers backing out.

When Poplar ends on Lagunitas Road, turn left. In 1 block make a right onto Shady Lane.

Along its short ½ mile, Shady Lane has four stop signs, one at each end and two in the middle. It also has two large STOP SIGN AHEAD signs. The sheriff of Ross has been known to hide in the bushes with a videocamera, taking pictures of bicyclists running stop signs. Mayors in Ross are elected on platforms of "Ending the Bicycle Problem." Ross is so antibike it lobbied to block the Bike Centennial Pacific Coast Route from passing through its hallowed streets. As a result, bicycle tourists laden with camping gear are directed by signs to take their chances on manic, narrow Sir Francis Drake. I don't even get surprised, let alone angry, when I am cut off, squeezed off the road, honked at, or physically intimidated by cars—usually expensive cars driven by successful people—in Ross.

At the last of Shady Lane's stop signs, turn right onto Bolinas Avenue. (*Note* that this Bolinas Avenue, unlike the Bolinas Avenue in Fairfax, does not turn into Bolinas-Fairfax Road if you turn west on it.) Head east 1 block. At the light turn left onto San Anselmo Avenue, which runs just this side of busy Sir Francis Drake.

San Anselmo features stop sign after stop sign, along with a few prominent BIKE ROUTE signs. Sometimes there are both signs on the same post, and in conspiracy-theorizing moods I wonder if a subliminal message is intended. But then, I wonder the same thing about trash cans at Disneyland emblazoned WASTE PLEASE.

Continue through all the stop signs until San Anselmo Avenue curves left and becomes Hazel Avenue. Follow a BIKE ROUTE sign here right back onto San Anselmo Avenue.

Soon San Anselmo becomes Forrest Avenue, but you can make a right turn and stay on San Anselmo. Do so. You'll come to a stop sign a few feet later. Turn left here onto Lansdale Avenue, which takes you into downtown Fairfax, gateway to rural West Marin.

All these turns may sound confusing, but the route is actually well marked with BIKE ROUTE signs, and after a few dozen times you'll have the route well memorized.

From Fairfax there are really two options, both leading to pretty good riding. One is to turn left onto Bolinas Avenue, which turns into Fairfax-Bolinas Avenue and climbs up to the Meadow Club, drops down the Alpine Dam, and then climbs up to Ridgecrest Drive on Mt.

Tam. For a route describing this road refer to the Alpine Dam Loop (Ride 22).

The other option is to take Sir Francis Drake north out of Fairfax and over White's Hill. Go this way if planning to ride the Cheese Factory Loop, the Olema Loop, or other routes of your own invention. I was thinking of including some of these wonderful routes in West Marin, out past White's Hill, but then I thought, why bother? All the roads are basically rural and lightly traveled; you can hardly go wrong. Just refer to a map and make up your own route. When you're done, follow this freeway route in reverse to return to San Francisco.

Headlands Loop

Number of miles:	7.6
Approximate pedaling time:	1 hour
Terrain:	Hilly
Traffic:	Light
Things to see:	Postcard views of the city and Golden Gate Bridge, Kirby Cove, abandoned batteries, Black Sand Beach, Point Bonita Lighthouse, Rodeo Lagoon, Headlands Institute for the Arts, horse stables

"I don't have time to get in shape." You hear it all the time. It's the biggest excuse people make for not riding enough.

I said it myself, once, to the wrong person: Elaine Mariolle. Mariolle, winner in record time of the Race Across America and author of *The Woman Cyclist*, replied in surprise, "You mean you couldn't spare an hour a day? People always say they don't have time, but really, it's a bad excuse. Anyone can find a few extra hours a week for something really important to them, and that's really all it takes."

She's right. And this loop ride is proof. Located just across the Golden Gate Bridge, it is easily accessible to San Francisco citizens, most of whom could, if they weren't so darn lazy, complete it and ride back home within an hour or two.

Don't just take my word for it. Try it for yourself. Take your usual route to the Golden Gate Bridge. After crossing the bridge ride to the west side and begin climbing Conzelman Road.

Postcard views of the city will ease your climbing agony during the first part of the climb, which is the steepest stretch on the loop. Once you round the first turn, you can take a dirt road to the left

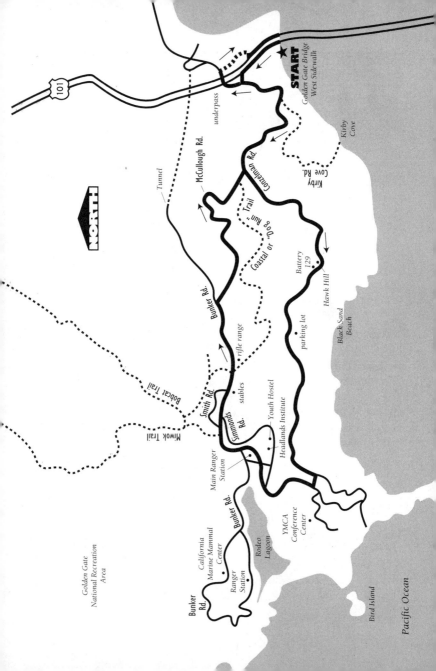

NORTH

Golden Gate National Recreation Area

Pacific Ocean

Bird Island

Bunker Rd.

California Marine Mammal Center

Ranger Station

Rodeo Lagoon

Bunker Rd.

Main Ranger Station

Simmonds Rd.

Smith Rd.

stables

Youth Hostel

Headlands Institute

YMCA Conference Center

Miwok Trail

Bobcat Trail

rifle range

Bunker Rd.

Tunnel

McCullough Rd.

"Dog Run"

Coastal or "Trail"

Conzelman Rd.

underpass

101

parking lot

Battery 129

Hawk Hill

Black Sand Beach

Kirby Cove

Kirby Cove Rd.

START

Golden Gate Bridge West Sidewalk

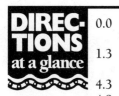

DIREC- TIONS at a glance

0.0 Starting at the west, Marin side of the Golden Gate Bridge, head uphill on Conzelman Road.

1.3 At intersection with McCullough Road, stay left on Conzelman.

4.3 Turn right sharply onto Field Road.

4.8 Turn right onto Bunker Road.

5.3 Turn right onto McCullough Road.

6.3 Turn left onto Conzelman Road to return to Golden Gate Bridge.

7.6 End at Golden Gate Bridge.

down to Kirby Cove, where you get a view of the city *underneath* the Golden Gate Bridge. Or shift up a few gears and continue winding around the southern cape of the Marin headlands on Conzelman.

Soon you'll come to an intersection. This is the beginning of the loop. Continue upward, staying left on Conzelman. A gate across the road here closes the road at night and in heavy fog.

When you get to the top of Hawk Hill, you'll find the remains of a battery where heavy artillery once perched to protect the Golden Gate from marine invasion. There were guns here that could heft a shell weighing as much as a Volkswagen Beetle accurately at distances up to 2 miles. If you have the time and inclination, a walk around the premises, with its numerous historical plaques, makes an interesting respite from the bicycle.

One plaque includes a picture of John Frémont, namer of the Golden Gate, who in 1846 sneaked across the bay from Sausalito, spiked the guns of Fort Winfield Scott, which was then called the Castillo de San Joaquin under Mexican rule, and raised the American flag without firing a shot. It was a rare episode of nonviolence for Frémont, whom history remembers in part for taking no prisoners. One of the "Pathfinder's" men reported in 1847: "We killed plenty of game and an occasional Indian. We made it a rule to spare none of the bucks."

Continuing on, the road becomes a very steep one-way drop

down to Black Sand Beach. Check your brakes before starting, and if it's foggy, hold the pads lightly against the rims to squeegee the rims dry before braking. Hang on, this one's STEEP!!!

Passing the parking lot to Black Sand, a semipopular nude beach, continue up a slight hill and around a few gentle curves. After passing through another road gate, turn right around a hairpin and continue on Field Road, unless you feel like exploring Point Bonita Lighthouse or going out to the YMCA camp, in which case take a left.

After passing between some abandoned military buildings, look to the left across Rodeo Lagoon. There you'll see the buildings of the California Marine Mammal Center—a hospice for injured sea lions that welcomes visitors and especially volunteers—and buildings of the Headlands Institute for Art (the main campus is just ahead). There is also a ranger station with interesting displays on local flora and fauna.

As you continue to descend into the Rodeo Valley, the temperature usually drops considerably. Soon you'll come to a cluster of buildings known as Fort Barry, which houses a youth hostel, more buildings of the Headlands Institute, and, on the left, the main ranger station for the headlands. Camping permits for the headlands can be obtained here. I particularly recommend spending a full-moon night at Hawk Camp, a two-site wilderness aerie far from the noises of civilization and accessible only by an off-road trail.

The Headlands Institute for Art, on the right, has the most spectacular bathroom I've ever seen anywhere. Check it out even if you don't really have to go. Especially note the noise the toilets make when flushed. As long as you're there, you might want to put your name on the mailing list. The Institute provides live-work grants and work studios to hundreds of artists, who occasionally put on absolutely amazing open studio and performance events. Cooking classes are also offered, some of which utilize an immense wood-fired brick oven.

Continuing on, make a right onto Bunker Road. Follow it as it begins to climb gradually. On the right you'll see a stable full of friendly horses. To the left, there are trailheads for the Bobcat and Miwok trails, the primary off-road thoroughfares through the headlands.

Soon, on the right, you'll see the rifle range, a field with little hills for leaning targets against. On the right edge of the range a dirt road, known informally as Dog Run or Lower Coastal Trail, leads back up to Conzelman Road. If you take it early in the morning, you'll often see a bluish-gray fox.

Continue on until a paved road ascends to the right. Here you can turn right on McCullough Road and climb back up to Conzelman, where you can turn right for another loop or left to coast down to the bridge.

Or, if you're too tired out for another climb, you can continue on Bunker Road. Soon you'll come to a narrow tunnel. Car traffic alternates directions every six minutes, but on a bicycle, you don't have to wait for the light. Merely push a button, and a sign will light up warning motorists of bicycles in the tunnel.

The tunnel runs significantly downhill as you head east, and hence is much more pleasant to ride out of than into the headlands. When you emerge, make two right turns and you'll find yourself back at the Golden Gate Bridge.

There you have it. The Headlands Loop. Now, what's your excuse?

Paradise Loop

Number of miles:	23.5 (36 round-trip from Golden Gate Bridge)
Approximate pedaling time:	3 hours
Terrain:	Rolling with one climb
Traffic:	Light except for Tamalpais Drive and East Blithedale Avenue
Things to see:	Max H. Graefe Wildlife Sanctuary, Richardson Bay, the Lyford House, Tiburon, views of the bay from a quiet shoreline road, a wooded climb

The Paradise Loop is the bread-and-butter training ride for many competitive cyclists in San Francisco. No other ride as close in to the city has as much to offer: quiet, scenic, sweet-smelling bayfront roads, one nice 400-foot climb, and the typically temperate weather of East Marin.

It isn't just a ride for racers, either. Hundreds of casual cyclists ride part or all of it every day. They appreciate the early bail-out options, one of which cuts the ride in half by incorporating a scenic ferryboat ride back to town.

Racers, being conscious of time, tend to ride the loop, um, clockwise. And they tend to cut out some of the scenic loops included here. Though these shortcuts are shown on the map, my version goes counterclockwise and throws in all the frills.

Begin at Bayfront Park in Mill Valley. For directions to the start from the Golden Gate Bridge, refer to the Marin Freeway route (Ride 18). From the Richardson Bay bike path, turn onto the Bay Front bike path, which immediately crosses a large wooden bridge. Continue on the path until it merges into Hamilton Drive. When Hamil-

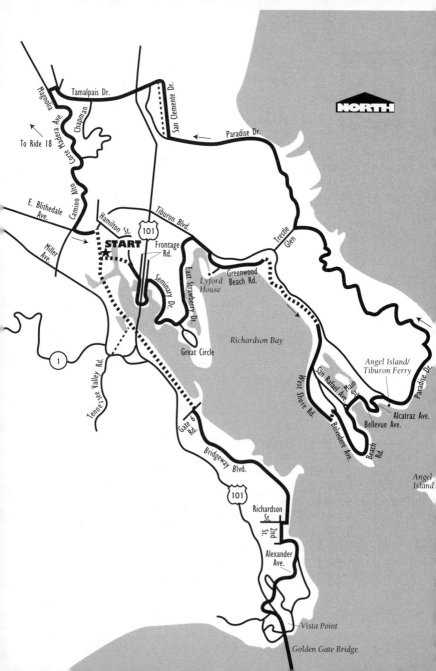

DIREC-TIONS
at a glance

0.0   Start by turning right off the Richardson Bay bike path onto the Bay Front Park bike path.

0.4   Turn right onto Hamilton Street bike path, which passes some DO NOT ENTER signs intended for cars.

0.8   Turn right onto Frontage Road.

1.3   Cross under freeway and head back in opposite direction.

1.6   Turn right onto Seminary Drive.

1.8   Bear right to stay on Seminary.

3.0   Stay left at Great Circle to stay on Seminary.

4.0   Seminary changes to East Strawberry Drive.

4.3   Turn right onto East Blithedale/Tiburon Boulevard.

4.4   Turn right onto Greenwood Beach Road.

4.9   Note Audubon Society's George Whittel Education Center, at 76 Greenwood Cove, and Lyford House behind it.

5.4   Greenwood Cove dead-ends. Continue through emergency vehicle passage marked by black-and-white striped curb. When you emerge, go right onto bike path.

5.5   Enter Richardson Bay Park.

6.7   Path ends on Tiburon Boulevard. Turn right onto San Rafael Avenue.

7.1   Turn right onto West Shore Road.

7.9   West Shore ends; take path left up very steep hill.

8.1   Continue on Belvedere Way.

8.3   Turn right onto Belvedere Avenue.

8.9   Stay right on Beach Road.

9.2   Stay right at roundabout to continue on Beach Road, which then becomes Main Street.

9.9   Turn right onto Bellevue Avenue.

10.2   Turn left onto Alcatraz Avenue.

10.3   Turn right onto Eastview Avenue.

10.4   Turn right onto one-way street.

10.5   Rejoin Main Street, which turns left.

10.6   Alley on right to Angel Island/Tiburon Ferry.

10.7 Turn right onto Paradise Drive.

10.9 Gate to Lyford's planned utopian community.

14.1 Marin County Public Beach Park to right.

16.1 Trestle Glen to left is a shortcut to Tiburon Boulevard near Blackie's Pasture.

19.2 At intersection with San Clemente Drive, pick up bike path to right.

19.7 Go left onto busy Tamalpais Drive. Merge left to avoid freeway entrance.

20.7 Turn left onto Corte Madera Avenue and begin climbing.

21.8 Summit of Corte Madera Ridge.

23.1 Turn left onto East Blithedale Avenue.

23.2 Turn right onto Richardson Bay bike path.

23.5 End at Bay Front Park.

---

ton ends on Frontage Road, take it right until it passes under the freeway and sends you back up the other side. Look for a right onto Seminary Drive.

Seminary Drive curves around scenic Harbor Point before turning into Strawberry Drive and ending at Tiburon Boulevard. Take Tiburon right for 1 block before making a right onto Greenwood Beach Drive.

A half-mile along Greenwood Cove, look for the beautiful Lyford house on the right. This stately three-story Victorian has been completely restored. It was built by Dr. Lyford, a wealthy mortician of the Civil War era who was the first to patent an embalming process that included instructions for the use of makeup to impart a lifelike appearance. Lyford was also a real estate developer who planned a utopian community called Lyford's Hygeia, named for the Greek goddess of health. Appropriately, the best part of this ride—the part on Paradise Drive—runs through the region he originally subdivided as Hygeia.

Continue on Greenwood until it ends and a multiuse path starts to the right, running along the bay. It continues a considerable distance before ending where San Rafael Avenue meets Tiburon Boulevard. Go right onto San Rafael Avenue, which leads down to Belvedere Island. Staying on San Rafael takes you along the northwest side of Belvedere, the most direct route to Tiburon. Our route makes a right onto West Shore Road to take in a tour of this island's shore and outrageous domiciles.

West Shore Road ends soon, but a very steep path to the left takes us up to Belvedere Way, which in turn leads to Belvedere Avenue, where we make a right. Belvedere Avenue soon makes a 180-degree turn and becomes Beach Road. Soon it rejoins San Rafael Avenue at a roundabout in front of the San Francisco Yacht Club; go right here to stay on Beach, which becomes Main Street.

Our route includes one last loop around scenic Corinthian Isle. Make a right onto Bellevue Avenue, a left onto Alcatraz Avenue, then two quick rights—one on Eastview and another on an unnamed one-way lane—before rejoining Main Street. Main then curves left into Tiburon's cute shop district. Just past the Cafe Sweden House Bakery, which has a nice outdoor pier seating section in back, look for a green sign on the right indicating the Angel Island/Tiburon Ferry terminal. Ferry boats run from here back to San Francisco and out to Angel Island, a large, nearly undeveloped island with a paved loop road and lots of hiking trails.

If you don't feel like taking the ferry back, make a right when Main Street ends onto Paradise Drive. The next 9 miles on Paradise are really the reason most people ride this loop. They are rolling, twisting, beautiful, and almost traffic-free, passing through the lightly developed Hill Haven, Belvedere Gardens, and Paradise Cay districts.

After about 5 miles, if you are getting tired, you can make a left onto Trestle Glen, which takes you back to Tiburon Boulevard and shortens the ride considerably. If you take this bail-out option, refer to the map for the route back to the Richardson Bay bike path. Otherwise, keep cruising until you see San Clemente Drive on the right. Make a right on the bike path parallel to San Clemente.

When the path ends, go left onto busy Tamalpais Drive. *Keep alert* as you merge to the left across the right lane, which becomes a freeway on-ramp. Climb up over the 101 freeway and stay on Tamalpais

as it takes you gradually uphill to Corte Madera. It will curve to the right and then to the left before intersecting Corte Madera Avenue, where you make a left and begin a 400-foot climb to the Camino Alto Preserve. At the summit Corte Madera Avenue becomes Camino Alto and descends to East Blithedale Avenue, where you make a left, and, in 1 block, a right onto the Richardson Bay bike path.

In less, than a mile, you'll be back in the Bay Front Park and you'll see the bike path you turned on earlier and took to Hamilton Road. Turn left here if you feel like going around another time. Otherwise, continue straight and follow the Marin Freeway route back to town.

There you have it, the Paradise Loop, with all the frills. May riding it put the rosy glow of good health into your cheeks.

Muir Woods Loop

Number of miles:	24
Approximate pedaling time:	2 hours
Terrain:	Hilly
Traffic:	*Bad on weekends!* Sketchy on beautiful weekdays. Best on days when San Francisco is fogbound and Marin is sunny.
Things to see:	Mill Valley, bay and ocean views, Muir Woods, Ralph Waldo Emerson Tree, Muir Beach, Green Gulch Farms, bay wetlands

This is a wonderful alternative to the Paradise Loop, if ridden at the right time. You've got to time this ride to miss traffic. On weekends or even on nice summer weekdays, there's too much congestion. On fall and spring weekdays, though, when fog is paralyzing the citizens of San Francisco and Marin is basking in sun, this ride is a real pleasure.

Start from the Miller Avenue exit of the Marin Freeway route (Ride 18). Take Miller into Mill Valley. When you get to The Depot, you may want to stop and hang out at The Depot, a popular meeting spot for Marin cyclists that features pleasant outdoor seating, coffee, pastries, and a bookstore. Continue by jogging left onto Sunnyside Avenue, right back onto Miller, then left onto Throckmorton.

Throckmorton curves to the right, and soon you'll see Old Mill Park to your left, erstwhile site of Mill Valley's eponymous sawmill. The lumber used to build the Presidio was taken from Corte Madera ("cut wood" in Spanish) and milled in Mill Valley.

You are about to begin a labyrinthine climb on a series of back streets, switchbacking up through mossy, damp residential areas.

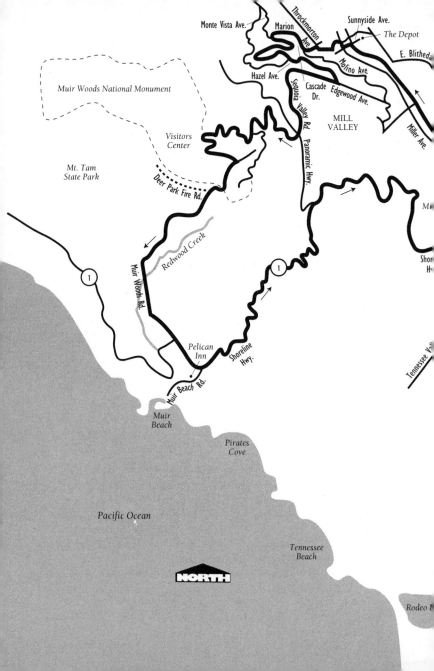

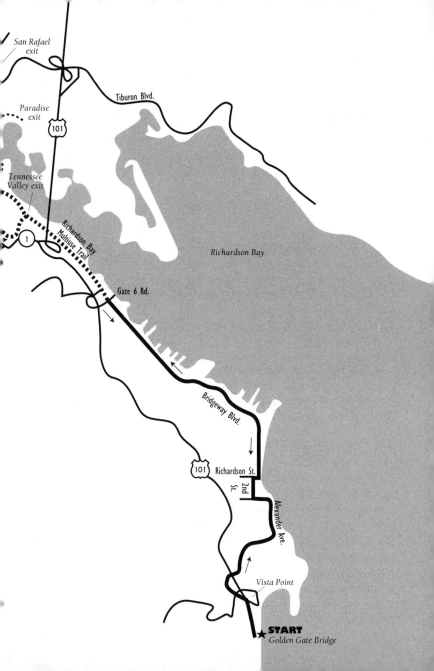

San Rafael exit

Tiburon Blvd.

Paradise exit

101

Tennessee Valley exit

1

Richardson Bay Multiuse Trail

Richardson Bay

Gate 6 Rd.

Bridgeway Blvd.

101 Richardson St.

2nd St.

Alexander Ave.

Vista Point

START
Golden Gate Bridge

DIREC-TIONS at a glance

0.0	Start at Golden Gate Bridge; follow Marin Freeway (Ride 18) directions to Miller Avenue exit.	
5.5	Exit Marin Freeway; turn right onto Miller Avenue.	
7.3	Turn left onto Sunnyside Avenue.	

7.4 Turn right onto Miller Avenue.

7.5 Turn left onto Throckmorton Avenue.

7.7 Turn left onto Cascade Way.

7.8 Turn right onto Molino Avenue.

7.9 Molino becomes Cascade Drive.

8.1 Turn left onto Marion Avenue.

8.4 Turn right onto Monte Vista Avenue.

8.6 Turn left onto Hazel Avenue.

8.9 Turn right onto Marion Avenue.

9.0 Turn right onto Edgewood Avenue.

9.4 Turn left onto Sequoia Valley Road.

10.1 Cross Panoramic Highway and continue straight onto Muir Woods Road.

12.3 Pass Old Mine Trail.

13.2 Turn left onto Shoreline Highway.

13.5 Pass Muir Beach Road, Pelican Inn to the right.

18.4 Turn right onto Miller Avenue.

18.6 Cross Miller (*be careful*) and pick up arched wooden bike bridge.

18.7 Turn left onto bike path after crossing steep wooden bridge.

18.9 Turn right onto Richardson Bay Multiuse Trail and follow Marin Freeway (Ride 18)

24.0 End at Golden Gate Bridge.

Even with a map it's easy to get lost, even after you've ridden this way a few times before. Take your time and *pay attention*!

Turn left into the park on Cascade Way, which is called Old Mill on the other side of Throckmorton. On the other side of the tiny park, turn right onto Molino. Molino soon changes names, becoming Cascade Drive. Take Cascade a short way before turning left onto Marion Avenue.

You could actually take Marion all the way up to Edgewood Avenue. However, I recommend turning right onto Monte Vista Avenue after ¼ mile. In another ¼ mile, turn left onto Hazel Avenue. Hazel takes you ½ mile to Edgewood.

Turn right onto Edgewood. Edgewood curves left at Castle Rock and changes names to Sequoia Valley Road. Continue climbing on Sequoia Valley Road until you come to a saddle, where you cross over busy Panoramic Highway and continue on Muir Woods Road. Got all that?

The intersection with Panoramic Highway is known as Four Corners. It is on a ridgeline and offers views of both the bay and, past Franks Valley, the Pacific Ocean. (This view is shown in the photograph on page 170.)

There is often a catering truck parked here, although you shouldn't count on it. The truck, when it's here, has an excellent selection of fresh bread, fresh and dried fruits, nuts, and cheeses. Most of the price signs include the words FUN TO EAT. For example, BREAD. FUN TO EAT. $2.99, or PEACHES. FUN TO EAT. 69¢/LB. Very few things at this catering truck are not touted as fun to eat.

The descent down Muir Woods Road is also fun, though not fun to eat. It is technical and smoothly paved. Wait for the cars and motorcycles to get about five minutes ahead or else you'll quickly catch up and have to ride down with the brakes clamped on. Or pass them.

This part of the ride passes through a small corner of Muir Woods, named, of course, for the great author and naturalist, founder of the Sierra Club, and inspiration behind our National Park system, John Muir. Muir actually had little connection with these woods, although he did run a fruit farm in the East Bay, over in Martinez, where he sometimes lived when not bundled up in a wool blanket in some nameless Sierra glacial crevasse.

The coastal redwoods in Muir Woods are magnificent, and they have been conveniently piped in for urban nature seekers to consume

167

en masse. A plaque on one particular redwood in the cathedral-like park has been dedicated to Ralph Waldo Emerson, who wrote in his essay, "Nature":

In the woods, is perpetual youth. Within these plantations of God, a decorum and sanctity reign, a perennial festival is dressed, and the guest sees not how he should tire of them in a thousand years. In the woods, we return to reason and faith. There I feel that nothing can befal me in life,— no disgrace, no calamity, (leaving me my eyes,) which nature cannot repair. Standing on the bare ground,—my head bathed by the blithe air, and uplifted into infinite space,—all mean egotism vanishes. I become a transparent eye-ball. I am nothing. I see all. The currents of the Universal Being circulate through me: I am part or particle of God.

Continuing past the trailhead marked Old Mine Trail but known to all mountain bikers as Deer Park, you'll come in a mile to an intersection with Shoreline Highway, Route 1. To the right it climbs up to a ridge that carries you high above the ocean a good way north. Our route goes left, however. Actually, it's more like going straight than left. In any case, *don't* turn right here.

Soon you'll see Muir Beach Road, on the right, and the Pelican Inn, a classy place to have a brew or two. Or make like a pelican and stuff your face.

Past the Pelican await the sands of Muir Beach, a small alcove in the coastal seawall with a spit of sand harboring a tiny lagoon. Here are port-o-potties and a delicious water fountain.

Continuing past Muir Beach Road, Shoreline Highway begins climbing. Note the bountiful fields of Green Gulch Farm below to the right, where Buddhist monks grow vegetables for Greens Restaurant at Fort Mason in San Francisco and herbs for Tassajara bread. They also offer Zen retreats at the farm. A trail past the fields leads up to the Green Gulch trails, among the most beautiful single tracks in Marin and now fully legal in the uphill direction!

Shoreline is very narrow, and a disconcerting guardrail hems you in as cars roar past up the moderate grade. If there's too much traffic, this climb isn't much fun. It doesn't last long, however, and soon you'll find yourself whizzing down the other side back down into Mill Valley. This descent is technical but nicely cambered and smoothly surfaced. It's almost impossible to ride without getting stuck behind cars, though. At the bottom it levels out a little, then breaks into civilization—a shopping center and several gas stations.

At the first light, where Almonte Avenue intersects Shoreline from the left, turn right to stay on Shoreline. Continue on Shoreline for ¹/₁₀ mile. Just before you cross a bridge, near a sign pointing to the right for Tennessee Valley Road, cross over busy Shoreline and pick up the arched, wooden bicycle-path bridge. Once over the bridge, the path turns left and takes you back to the main Marin Freeway route (Ride 18).

If bad traffic makes crossing Shoreline seem like an impossible ambition, continue on Shoreline over the bridge and turn right into the parking lot at the top of Tennessee Valley Road. Here you'll usually find Kevin the don't-panic-go-organic man with his mobile produce shop. Working outdoors keeps Kevin's overhead low.

Past Kevin's stand there's a little trail leading down to another trail next to the river, which you can follow under the bridge. *Watch out* for trolls, and the low pipe on the far side. Once you're back out in the light of day, pick up the bicycle path, head east (go straight—*don't* cross the wooden bridge), and pretty soon you'll be back on the main bicycle freeway route.

There you have it, the Muir Woods Loop. A nice two-to-three-hour escape into the decorum and sanctity of nature—when the tourist masses are elsewhere. When the tourists are thick, it's best avoided. All in all, a fitting honorarium to the somewhat misanthropic Muir, who gave up on humanity at age thirty to study the plant world, writing something to the effect of, "If not for this thing bread, I doubt the human race would see my face again."

Alpine Dam Loop

Number of miles:	42.4 round-trip from Golden Gate Bridge
Approximate pedaling time:	4 hours (from Golden Gate Bridge)
Terrain:	Mountainous, 3,300 cumulative elevation gain
Traffic:	Mostly light
Things to see:	Alpine Lake, Bolinas Ridge, Mt. Tam, hang gliders

The Alpine Dam loop is a real treat. It is my favorite short ride in Marin, and I know I'm not alone. Sometimes you see more bikes than cars on the stretch from Fairfax to Bolinas Ridge. I've seen Tinker Juarez up there three times, always in the big chainring, always carrying that backpack full of what looks suspiciously like rocks.

Even on the busiest weekend traffic day you'll see few cars along this ride. The hills are steep but partially shaded, so it isn't too bad on hot days. Oftentimes Ridgecrest will be shrouded in fog, and the bay and eucalyptus trees alongside the road collect moisture until they drip cloud-forest rain onto the roadway.

On clear summer days you'll probably see hang gliders off Ridgecrest. When you get to the top of Ridgecrest, an optional side trip up to the top of Mt. Tam adds about 3 miles and 600 feet of climbing—and unequaled panoramic views of Marin.

Finally, the descent is technical, smoothly paved, and, if you wait until there aren't any cars to slow you down, quite fast. In short, this ride starts off strenuous, gets picturesque, and finishes up exhilarating. What more could you ask from a loop ride a few miles from one of America's major cities?

The first step is to follow the Marin Freeway route (Ride 18) to

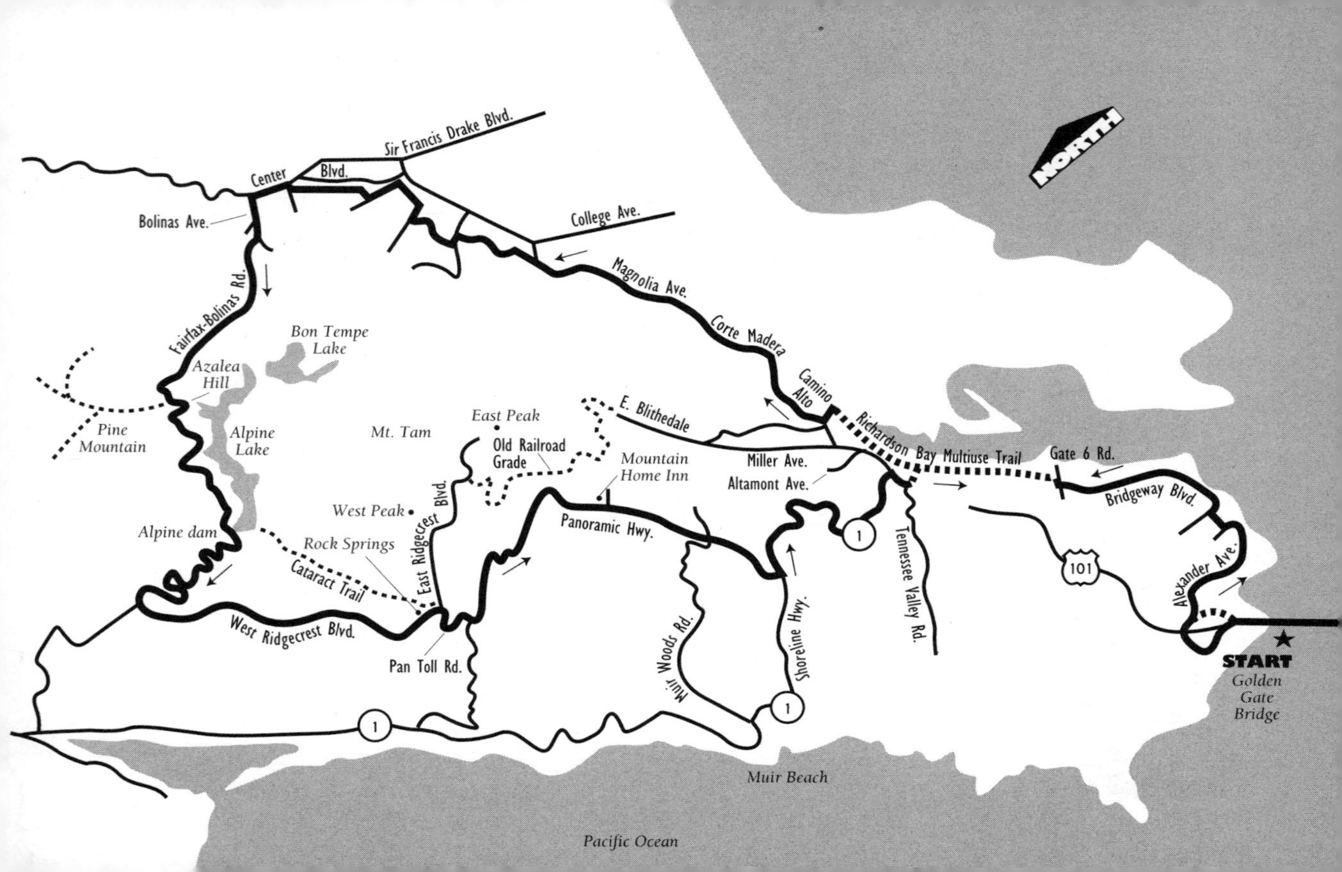

START
Golden Gate Bridge

Alexander Ave.

Bridgeway Blvd.

Gate 6 Rd.

101

Tennessee Valley Rd.

1

Richardson Bay Multiuse Trail

Camino Alto

Miller Ave.

Altamont Ave.

Shoreline Hwy.

1

Muir Beach

Pacific Ocean

Corte Madera

Magnolia Ave.

College Ave.

E. Blithedale

Mountain Home Inn

Panoramic Hwy.

Muir Woods Rd.

Sir Francis Drake Blvd.

East Peak

Old Railroad Grade

East Ridgecrest Blvd.

Pan Toll Rd.

1

Center Blvd.

Bon Tempe Lake

Mt. Tam

West Peak

Rock Springs

Cataract Trail

West Ridgecrest Blvd.

Bolinas Ave.

Fairfax-Bolinas Rd.

Azalea Hill

Alpine Lake

Alpine dam

Pine Mountain

DIREC-TIONS at a glance

0.0   From Golden Gate Bridge, follow Marin Freeway route (Ride 18) to Fairfax.

18.0   Turn left onto Bolinas Avenue, which becomes Fairfax-Bolinas Road.

25.7   Turn left onto West Ridgecrest Boulevard.

28.8   Rock Springs; turn left on East Ridgecrest Boulevard to summit of Mt. Tam, otherwise turn right onto Pan Toll Road.

34.9   Four Corners; continue through intersection.

36.8   Turn left onto Shoreline Highway—Route 1.

37.0   Turn right at Altamont Avenue to stay on Route 1.

37.1   Cross to east side of Route 1 and find bike path; continue over steep wooden bridge.

37.2   Turn left onto bike path just past steep wooden bridge.

37.4   Turn right onto Richardson Bay Multiuse Trail and follow Marin Freeway route (Ride 18) to Golden Gate Bridge.

42.4   Finish at Golden Gate Bridge.

Fairfax. The distance from the Golden Gate Bridge is about 18 miles and involves 660 feet of climbing. Once in Fairfax, turn left onto Bolinas Road.

In a few blocks, on the right, you'll see the site of the former Fat Tire Trading Post, the original Marin County mountain bike shop. It is still a bike shop but now has a different name.

Shortly past there you'll see the town park on the right, and a little bit farther you need to veer left to stay on Bolinas.

Bolinas wends up through residential neighborhoods before breaking free into open space and changing names to Fairfax-Bolinas Road. Some locals call it Bo-Fax Road. What a blessing it is that it has such a workmanlike name: Lots more tourists would drive it were it called Paradise or Nirvana or maybe Cloud Forest Mountain Lake Road or something.

Bo-Fax climbs gradually and persistently from 230 feet in Fairfax, past the parking lot for the Meadow Country Club and Golf Course, up to 1,140 feet at the trailhead for the Pine Mountain Offroad Loop, which goes off to the right (the path on the left leads to Azalea Hill). Bo-Fax then drops down past Alpine Lake to Alpine Dam, which it crosses over at mile $6^3/_{10}$.

Just past the dam is a trailhead for the Cataract Trail, definitely one of Marin's prettiest walks just after rainfall, when countless waterfalls tumble down the mountain's steep north side.

From here the word is *up*, and steeply so. Some racers time themselves from the Dam up to Rock Springs Gate, with thirty minutes considered to be okay and twenty-eight minutes being a good day.

The switchbacks here and the forest cover make for pure bliss— or agony—depending on whether or not you consider yourself a climber.

At $7^7/_{10}$ miles you're through with the steepest part as you meet up with Ridgecrest Road. A left here sends you continuing up Mt. Tam rather than dropping via a roughly paved minor back road into Stinson Beach.

If you do ride down to Stinson and back up on Bo-Fax Road before continuing on and finishing up this ride, you will have done the "Tam-and-a-half" ride, as some like to call it.

There is also a trailhead at the intersection of Ridgecrest and Bo-Fax roads for the Bolinas Ridge mountain bike trail, a scenic, rugged double track with perhaps more forest cover than any other trail in Marin. Don't try to ride it by moonlight!

Continuing on up Ridgecrest, look to your right for hang gliders plying the coastal thermals, or parked in lots alongside the road discussing life insurance policies.

At mile $10^3/_{10}$ the road tops out, and $3/_{10}$ mile later you pass through the gate at Rock Springs. A sign here indicates that the elevation is 1,940 feet. The cumulative gain so far will be 2,520, not including the 670 feet from the Golden Gate Bridge to Fairfax.

At Rocksprings you can decide whether to continue up to the top of Tam. Along with views of spiritual proportion, you'll find a snack shop that stocks yogurt, sodas, and postcards, an old fire lookout accessible via a short hike, and a fantastic foot trail circumnavigating the summit with 360-degree views. If you brought a lock, take the walk. It's cool. Elevation atop the East Peak is 2,571 feet above sea level.

Back down at Rock Springs, take note of the Mountain Theater, the summertime weekend host to regular dramatic performances. A knoll just west of the theater is a popular spot for weddings.

Continue down the mountain on Southside Road, also called Pan Toll Road. After descending for about a mile, make a left onto Panoramic and continue to descend. *Be wary* of hairpin rights.

After another 4$\frac{4}{10}$ miles notice the Mountain Home Inn on the left. Near here on the left you'll find trailheads for one of Marin's few remaining legal single tracks, the Tenderfoot, as well as for the Gravity Car connector trail to Railroad Grade.

In another 1$\frac{7}{10}$ miles, Panoramic arrives at an intersection known as Four Corners. Taking a left onto Sequoia Valley Road, which becomes Edgewood, and then a left onto Marion Avenue provides a scenic drop into Mill Valley, but our route takes the shortest way back, continuing on Panoramic another $\frac{7}{10}$ mile before going left onto Shoreline Highway. Continue descending on Shoreline until you see a big shopping center on the right and then arrive at Altamont Avenue. Turn right onto Altamont, then cross over to the other side, *being careful* of traffic, and pick up a bike path that crosses over Coyote Creek on a steep, narrow, wooden bridge. Go left onto the bike path after the bridge, then right after $\frac{2}{10}$ mile onto the Sausalito bike path.

From here refer to the Marin Freeway route (Ride 18) for directions to your starting point in Fairfax or back to the Golden Gate Bridge. In a nutshell, to get back to the bridge, take this path to the right until it ends at Sausalito Cyclery on Gate Six Road. Go right onto Gate Six and immediately left onto Bridgeway Boulevard, which will take you through scenic Sausalito. Then go right onto Richardson up a short steep hill, left onto Second Street up a more gradual hill, then left onto Alexander Avenue, which climbs back up to the bridge.

China Camp Agnolo

Number of miles:	25.7, or 38 round-trip from Golden Gate Bridge
Approximate pedaling time:	3 hours
Terrain:	Rolling hills, two 400-foot climbs on return leg
Traffic:	Heavy to light
Things to see:	windsurfers, San Quentin State Prison, McNears Beach, China Camp State Park, China Camp Village, Marin Civic Center, Bon Air Center, Corte Madera Creek

You may be wondering, after reading the title to this ride, what exactly an *agnolo* is. I have often been accused of being a Philadelphia lawyer (a person who uses fancy words), but you are not likely to find *agnolo* in the dictionary. It is too obscure a word for that. From the context, one might assume that an agnolo is some sort of excursion or trip, perhaps a circuit or a tour. In fact, however, that is not the case. In actuality, *agnolo* is a word used in order to determine if a reader is paying attention, as in the sentence, "My bicycle components are from Camp Agnolo." Now does it make sense?

You'll want to pay attention to this ride, because it features some nifty routes, including one between San Rafael and Larkspur that is virtually free of traffic and very scenic. About half of the miles in this ride are strikingly gorgeous. The other half aren't. The good half of the ride is so good, however, that it makes the whole thing definitely worthwhile.

The road through China Camp State Park, though fairly short, ranks among the best cycling roads of East Marin. The trails within

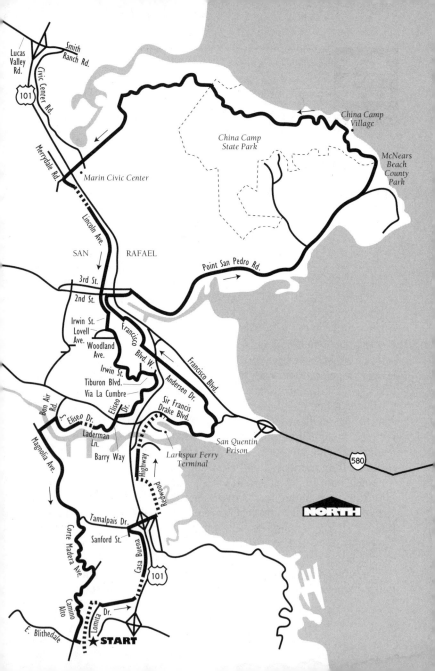

DIREC-TIONS at a glance

0.0 Start at East Blithedale and Richardson Bay bike path. Head north on the bike path.

0.4 Turn right onto small exit off path, pass school, and then continue on Lomita Drive.

1.0 Turn left onto bike path next to freeway.

1.4 Exit bike path; continue next to freeway on Casa Buena Drive.

2.4 Turn right onto Sanford Street.

2.5 Turn right onto Tamalpais Drive; cross freeway.

2.7 Turn left onto bike path along Redwood Highway.

3.8 Path ends; continue right on Redwood Highway.

4.2 Multiuse path starts on left.

4.3 Turn right onto shoulder sidewalk of freeway off-ramp/bridge.

4.5 Turn right onto bike path along Sir Francis Drake Boulevard.

4.9 Bike path ends; continue on Sir Francis Drake.

5.7 Turn left onto Andersen Drive.

6.3 Cross busy Bellam Boulevard.

6.7 Curve left at freeway entrance; Andersen becomes Francisco Boulevard West.

7.6 Turn right onto Second Street.

7.9 Second Street curves left, becomes Third Street.

8.2 Third Street becomes Point San Pedro Road.

10.8 Pass McNears Beach County Park.

11.1 Enter China Camp State Park.

16.5 Marin Civic Center on right.

17.0 Turn left onto Merrydale Road, first left after crossing under freeway.

17.1 Turn left onto bike path along freeway.

17.4 Turn left when path ends at Lincoln Avenue.

19.2 Turn right onto Irwin Street.

19.4 Turn left onto Lovell Avenue.

19.5 Cross Woodland Avenue; Lovell becomes Irwin Street.

20.7 Turn right onto Tiburon Boulevard. This becomes Via La Cumbre.

20.8 Continue on Via La Cumbre.

21.2 Turn left onto Eliseo Drive.
21.3 Cross Sir Francis Drake; Eliseo becomes Barry Way.
21.4 Turn right onto Laderman Lane.
21.6 Turn left onto bike path.
21.8 Turn left onto South Eliseo Drive.
22.4 Turn left onto Bon Air Road.
22.6 Turn left onto Magnolia Avenue.
25.6 Turn left onto East Blithedale Avenue.
25.7 End at Blithedale/Richardson Bay bike path.

---

the park offer a rare opportunity for Bay Area mountain bikers to ride single track legally: More than a dozen miles of very well-groomed, though heavily cross-trenched, single track are officially open to bikes.

This ride starts from Mill Valley and shoots up to San Rafael, where it encircles China Camp State Park before cutting through San Rafael to Corte Madera, going over the grade, and returning to Mill Valley. On the way to China Camp, it goes right past the Larkspur Ferry Terminal on Sir Francis Drake Boulevard, and on the way back it passes within ½ mile of the terminal. That means that road riders who want a shorter loop, and off-road cyclists wishing to save some pavement wear on their knobbies, can take the ferry to or from San Francisco in one or both directions and end up with a much shorter ride. For information about ferry service, contact Golden Gate Ferry Service at (415) 923–2000.

To get to the start of this ride, take the Marin Freeway route (Ride 18) to where the Richardson Bay bike path meets East Blithedale Avenue in Mill Valley. There, instead of following the freeway route (Ride 18) left on East Blithedale, cross East Blithedale and continue on the bike path for ½ mile. Look for a small bike path leading off the path to the right. This exit path goes past a school and lets you out on Lomita Drive.

Lomita climbs up gently toward the freeway, where a bike path starts to the left. This path fronts the freeway for a short distance before ending on Casa Buena Drive, where you should go right and continue north.

When Casa Buena ends on Sanford, go right and then make an immediate right onto Tamalpais Drive and cross over the freeway. Once on the other side, pick up the bike path along the Redwood Highway and continue north. After about a mile the path ends and you have to ride on Redwood Highway for ½ mile. Look for a multi-use path on the left, which puts you on the shoulder of a freeway off-ramp that carries you over Corte Madera Creek. From there, take a right onto the bike path along Sir Francis Drake Boulevard.

Note the ferry terminal on the right. Its geometrical roof always reminds me of one of those tetra-kites; I expect it to take off and fly away at any minute in the strong bay winds, probably taking the station with it.

Past the ferry terminal the bike path ends at a small park with a pond and signs explaining the wildlife. Also notice the old brick oven on the left, an ancient wood and sheet-metal building with an immense brick chimney.

Continue east on the wide, bike-lane shoulder of Sir Francis Drake. If the day is windy, you are likely to see windsurfers parked on the shoulder here and sailing down in the bay below. A little farther up on the right sprawls the high-security expanse of San Quentin State Prison. I wonder how the inmates of San Quentin feel, looking out over the bay at the ostentatious freedom of the windsurfers.

San Quentin, a high-security facility, has a lot of history. Its yellow walls have seen murders, riots, break-outs, and more than 400 state executions since it was built in the 1860s.

A little past San Quentin you'll see Andersen Drive on the left. Here, you have a choice. You could make a left onto Andersen and follow it down into San Rafael. It goes through a couple of busy intersections and twists around a little bit but eventually takes you to Second Street, where you can make a right and head on out of town. It is slightly shorter, and slightly less aesthetic, than the other option.

Your other choice is to continue on Sir Francis Drake until it puts you on the shoulder of the freeway. Take the first exit and cross under the freeway (the road to the right dead-ends at the gatehouse to San Quentin, near the San Quentin Handicraft Shop that sells items made by prisoners). Then make a left onto Francisco Boulevard, a fairly busy industrial-park sort of road, taking it north until you can make a right onto Second Street and head on out of town.

After a few blocks, Second Street, which is one-way, curves left and joins forces with Third Street. A few blocks farther, Third Street becomes Point San Pedro Road, and it isn't long after that that the road opens up to a view of the bay and the point itself, where you can see the brick chimneys of the McNears Brick Ovens. Traffic remains fairly steady, and the shoulder is narrow in places. *Take care.*

Past the point, McNears Beach County Park awaits. On sunny days lots of people pay to lie out here. It'll cost you $2.00 if you arrive by bicycle. The beach area is sheltered from the fog and features nicely groomed lawns, a couple of swimming pools, tennis courts, and a small restaurant/snack shop.

Just a little past McNears Beach County Park, China Camp State Park begins. The road narrows, but traffic drops considerably, too. A series of dramatic bay views, voluptuous rolling hills, open meadows with strong winds, and wooded points can inspire cyclists into a reverie of motion, but do make time for a stop at China Camp Village, a spot with a lot of history. Chinese men (few women came to America, initially) left unemployed by restrictive labor laws and the completion of the railroads came here by the hundreds in the late 1800s. Grass shrimp caught here were dried and shipped around the world. Many were sold on the streets of San Francisco. The chorus of Chinese shrimp vendors reverberates through the Victorian corridors of San Francisco history.

Finally, in 1910, a law against shrimp nets prompted the exit of most China Camp fishermen. Many buildings remain, however, along with gravelly beaches, a drying pier, a few old boats, and an ancient lunch counter where you can still get clam chowder and other fruits of the bay.

Past China Camp, Point San Pedro Road turns a corner and tends to develop a headwind. Five miles later it arrives at the Marin Civic Center, an aqueduct-looking structure designed by Frank Lloyd Wright that houses the courts and county offices of Marin. When you arrive here, you may wish to turn around and ride back to the other side of China Camp. In fact, you may want to ride back and forth several times, enjoying this excellent road. Another way to extend your ride would be to take Civic Center Road north to Smith Ranch Road. A left there takes you out of town on Lucas Valley Road. From there make a left onto Nicasio Valley Road, then a left onto Sir Francis Drake, and you'll be in Fairfax, from where you can follow the Marin Freeway route back to the city.

Back on the main route, continue past the Civic Center on Point San Pedro and cross underneath the 101 freeway. Make the first left, ignoring the NOT A THROUGH STREET sign. At the top of a short climb, continue next to the freeway on the bike path. When the path ends, make a left onto Lincoln Avenue and continue down a long, gentle grade.

Soon you'll pass through downtown San Rafael, where lots of shops and restaurants beckon. A few blocks farther, look for a right turn onto Irwin Street.

Irwin turns into Lovell briefly, before becoming itself again and beginning a climb. Stay to the right as Rose and Altena Street drop to the left. Stay on the main road as it changes names from Irwin to Tiburon Boulevard to Via La Cumbre. It splits in several places, offering dramatically sweeping rollers that are fun to try to keep momentum on. This is a neat road, but *be careful* of people backing out of driveways!

Soon Via La Cumbre becomes extremely steep and ends at Eliseo Drive. Go left here and cross over busy Sir Francis Drake. Note that Larkspur Ferry Terminal is on Drake about ¼ mile to the left. On the other side of Drake, continue down a small street called Barry Way, which leads past an entrance to the Bon Air Center shopping mall.

A short distance past the Bon Air Center, make a right onto Laderman Lane. When Laderman curves away to the right, continue straight on a short bike path next to Corte Madera Creek. Soon this path ends at South Eliseo Drive, where you should go left.

South Eliseo eventually ends at Bon Air Road. Cross over Bon Air and make a left onto the bike lane, which has its own lane of the bridge over Corte Madera Creek. A short distance later, Bon Air meets Magnolia. Turn left here and continue, through Corte Madera, up and over the Corte Madera Grade, and down Camino Alto to East Blithedale. A left onto East Blithedale brings you in 1 block to the Richardson Bay bike path and the start of the ride.

The Freeway South

Number of miles:	21.2
Approximate pedaling time:	2 hours
Terrain:	Hilly, 1,250 feet of climbing
Traffic:	Variable; less than on El Camino
Things to see:	Ridgeline views of bay and ocean, Crystal Springs Reservoir, San Andreas dam and lake, Sawyer Camp Bicycle Trail

When riding south from San Francisco, there are two options, really, besides the route described in SFO Ramble (Ride 15). You can take the high road or the low road. The high road consists mainly of Skyline Boulevard, which this ride describes. The low road mainly follows Valencia Street, Mission Street, and El Camino Real, which are often quite busy. Actually, once you get to Burlingame, you can turn left off ECR onto Bayswater Avenue (pronounced Bay Swatter), then turn right onto Dwight Road, which becomes Delaware Street, which is mellower. El Camino is definitely not mellow. It is often congested and unpleasant. It is, however, flat and fast. If you have the time, the high road—Skyline—is a better option.

Skyline, as its name might suggest, is not flat, although it doesn't present any really long climbs until just after where this route leaves off, south of Sawyer Camp Bicycle Trail. There are places where Skyline Boulevard is sort of unpleasant and freewaylike, but it never gets as bad as El Camino Real. Many people commute along it on bicycles every day. It offers pleasant views on clear days of both ocean and bay, a good supply of fresh ridge-top air, and a series of big rolling hills that are outright fun when it comes down to it.

This ride starts just west of Lake Merced, at the intersection of

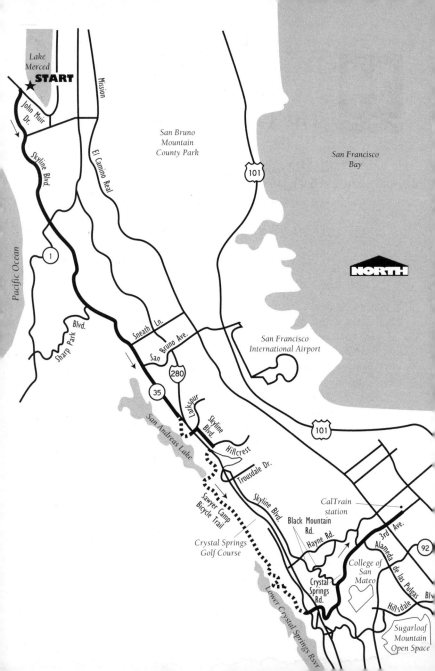

DIREC-TIONS at a glance

0.0	Start on Skyline Boulevard at John Muir Drive, just west of Lake Merced.
1.3	Cross San Mateo county line.
2.0	Pass John Daly Boulevard on left.
4.4	Merge left, following signs to Highway 35.
4.8	Merge to right after on-ramp.
4.9	Pacifica town limit sign.
6.9	Pass Sharp Park Boulevard on right (San Bruno city limit).
7.0	Follow narrow road for 400 yards.
10.0	Turn right onto bike path just before Skyline merges with 280 freeway.
11.1	Turn left onto Larkspur; cross under bridge.
11.2	Turn right onto Skyline Boulevard.
11.7	Turn right onto Hillcrest; cross under freeway.
11.8	Turn left onto Sawyer Camp Bicycle Trail.
17.8	Trail ends. Cross Skyline Boulevard and continue on Crystal Springs Road.
20.3	Turn right onto Third Avenue.
21.2	CalTrain station on left.

Skyline Boulevard and John Muir Drive. You can get to the start by riding out to Ocean Beach and turning south onto the Great Highway. When the Great Highway ends on Skyline at Lake Merced, turn right and continue ½ mile to the start.

You could also get to the ride by following Market Street west until Seventeenth Street. Turn right there, then left onto Corbett Avenue. When Corbett ends, merge right onto Market and continue climbing until it turns into Portola Drive and cruises downhill for a mile or so. When you get to Sloat Boulevard, turn right, then left when Sloat ends. A bit away from there, a right onto Skyline puts you on the route.

The route begins with an 800-foot climb up to Daly City on Skyline Boulevard. The climb is divided into three parts by two flat bits, and some call it the triple ripple. At the top Skyline crosses over

Route 1, the coastal highway. Here you'll have to merge left across an exit for Route 1 and then, a short distance later, merge right across two lanes of on-ramp.

Be sure to learn the safe technique for crossing lanes of freeway speed traffic. Here it is: Look physically over your shoulder several times as you approach the split. Wait until the last possible minute and then cut diagonally across the lane. When you are across, turn right and continue on the shoulder. Do not put yourself out in high-speed traffic by heading for the apex of the V. Inattentive drivers often veer wildly across several lanes of traffic to take an exit they were unprepared for. *Don't* be in their way.

After you've crossed lanes, look to the right out over the town of Pacifica to the Pacific Ocean. Next up are a series of rolling hills. Two miles farther you'll come to the town of San Bruno and an intersection with Sharp Park Boulevard. Sharp Park was reconstructed in the early 1990s with a generous bicycle lane. It is now a fine cycling road in both directions. At its terminus are a beautiful golf course and beach walk, as well as an archery range run by the city of San Francisco and the loving labor of its caretakers. For more details refer to the Planet of the Apes Road (Ride 12).

After Sharp Park the shoulder narrows for 100 yards. Then after Sneath Lane it narrows for 50 yards. After you pass Sneath Lane, the weather often changes from wind and fog to heat and sunlight as you cross over the spine of the peninsula.

Shortly after Sneath, Skyline descends for 2 blocks, climbs for 1 block, and then merges onto the 280 freeway. Bicyclists are required to exit and take the recreational bike path to the right. I wouldn't recommend taking the path at night, however. It's creepy. There are fences on both sides of the path and no lights. Ride the 280 freeway and take the first exit instead.

At the end of the path, you'll exit onto Larkspur Drive, which you should take under the freeway. Turn right past there and you'll be back on Skyline. In 1 block you'll turn right onto Hillcrest Boulevard, where you must decide whether to take the Sawyer Camp Bicycle Trail or continue on Skyline.

Since this ride is called the Freeway South, we should really stick to the faster route on Skyline, but just in case you have the time, I'll describe the Sawyer Camp Bicycle Trail first.

This trail can be very enjoyable and is much flatter than the Skyline route. It is a beautifully maintained, narrow path winding for 6 miles through dense forest, past San Andreas Lake and Lower Crystal Springs Reservoir. The trail begins by descending to San Andreas Dam, an earthen dam built in 1869. It continues past a golf course, then through dense foliage. It features many good smells and cool air seeping up from the reservoirs. All in all, it's very pleasant going.

As might be imagined based on all that, it's wildly popular and often totally packed, at least for the first mile or so at each end. *Do be careful* of dogs, dog leashes, baby carriages, skaters, walkers, and other trail users. Eventually you'll wind back up a little hill and emerge out onto Skyline Boulevard again.

Now for the freeway version. Instead of the path, turn left from Hillcrest onto a freeway on-ramp. Ride the shoulder until the next exit. Then cross under the freeway and make the first right, onto Skyline Boulevard.

For a few miles you'll continue on Skyline as it runs along the east side of the 280 corridor.

At Black Mountain Road there's a shortcut to San Mateo called the Tartan Trail. It is very steep but saves a stitch in time over Skyline to Crystal Springs.

Another useful shortcut is to follow Black Mountain Road to Hayne Road. Turn right onto Hayne Road; then merge left onto El Cerrito Avenue, which becomes Tilton Avenue and carries you under the CalTrain tracks and onto a spiral overpass over the 101 freeway. Continuing on Monte Diablo to the bayfront bike path, you can pick up the Foster City Flats route (Ride 13).

The main route turns right here, passing a freeway entrance and crossing below the 280. Rather than turning right onto Golf Course Road, turn left and continue on Skyline Boulevard, which drops down some stair-stepping rollers before passing the southern terminus of the Sawyer Camp Trail, where there are always lots of cars parked.

Just past the trailhead you can continue on Skyline—which gets hillier from here on out—or turn left onto Crystal Springs Road, a gentle descent into San Mateo.

Once in San Mateo, turn right onto Third Avenue and follow it to the CalTrain station, just past B Street on the left side.

Soon you'll pass the CalTrain station, the train tracks, and, a short way later, Delaware Street.

The ride back to San Francisco currently costs around $2.50. Bicycles are allowed on cars with a yellow bicycle sign next to the door, usually the northernmost car. The number to call to find out when the next train will come is (800) 660–4287.

Should you decide to retrace your route and ride back to the city via this route, there are a few things to keep in mind. As you near San Francisco on Skyline Boulevard/Highway 35, you'll cross over Highway 1. This interchange requires merging left across several lanes of fairly fast traffic. *Be careful here.*

There you have it. The first segment of the Freeway South. It isn't all sun and games. But even at rush hour it's not so bad, really. I rode it several hundred times during two years of working down in Foster City.

And when you're looking for some truly awesome riding, try some of the rides just south of this ride. Instead of turning left onto Crystal Springs, continue south, turn left onto Cañada Road, and continue down to Palo Alto. Or you can climb up to the peninsular ridge by making a right onto Highway 92 and then a left onto Highway 35.

Skyline and the roads that branch off it south of Highway 92 are beautiful, forested, dramatic byways, some of the most popular cycling roads in the country, in fact. But that's another story. And you don't need me to tell you where to ride down there. There are already tons of guidebooks covering the area.

Appendix

This appendix lists the transit services in the San Francisco area that allow bicycles on the transit system, when they are allowed, and what restrictions and limitations apply. Bicyclists wishing to cross San Francisco Bay can take advantage of the Bicycle Commuter Shuttle, which carries passengers across the San Francisco/Oakland Bay bridge during commuting hours on weekdays (call 510–286–0669). Limited shuttle service is provided by Cal-Trains maintenance vehicles on the San Mateo/Hayward and Carquinez bridges (call 510–286–0589), and a daily shuttle service across the Benicia/Martinez bridge is also available (call 510–680–4636).

Bicycles on Bay Area Transit

Agency	Information
AC Transit	Exterior racks with space for two bikes on routes, F, N, O, and S; all buses, all hours. Bikes allowed inside buses on weekends only, all hours, on lines 65 and 67. For information call (510) 817–1717 or (510) 839–2882.
Alameda Harbor Ferry	Bikes allowed on a first-come, first-serve basis. For information call (510) 769–5500 or (415) 247–1604.
Alameda-Oakland Ferry	Bikes allowed on a first-come, first-serve basis. Up to twenty-five bikes can be accommodated. For information call (510) 522–3300.
Amtrak	Roll-on service on routes featuring the "California Cars," including the Capitol Corridor between San Jose and Sacramento. Cyclists may board at any station on these routes and hang their bikes (tandems do not fit) with bags removed on racks in the platform level baggage area of the double-deck coaches. On routes without California Cars, bikes are allowed only in boxes as baggage, where such service exists. The program is being implemented and may not be available on all trains. For more information on bicycle access, consult the California Association of Bicycling Organization's (CABO) publication *Wheels on Wheels*; or phone (510) 828–5299. For Amtrak routes and schedules, call (800) USA-RAIL.
Amtrak ThruWay Buses	From the Capitol Corridor route, Amtrak ThruWay buses will carry two to three bikes in the cargo bay as space is available. For information call (800) USA-RAIL.
BART	Bikes allowed in the rear of each car, but not in the lead car. Bike access on BART on weekdays is limited. Weekend and holiday access is unrestricted.
BART Express Buses	Bikes allowed onboard only during non-commute hours, per the driver's discretion. For information call (510) 465–2278.
Benicia Transit	Exterior racks with space for two bikes available on some buses, all hours. If rack is full or bus doesn't have a rack, one bike is allowed inside with front wheel removed. For information call (707) 422–BUSS.
Blue & Gold Ferry	Bikes allowed on a first-come, first-serve basis. Up to twenty-five bicycles can be accommodated. For information call (415) 705–5555.

CalTrain	Up to twenty-four bikes allowed inside the northernmost car (San Francisco end of train) of all trains at all times. Some trains reach capacity. For information call (800) 660–4287.
County Connection (Contra Costa)	Exterior racks with space for two bikes on most buses. Two bikes may also be taken inside buses, depending on passenger load. Cyclists age twelve and under must be accompanied by an adult. For information call (925) 676–7500.
Dumbarton Express	Exterior racks with space for two bikes on all buses, all hours. One bike may also be taken inside buses, depending on passenger load. For information call (510) 471–2498.
Fairfield/Suisun Transit	Exterior racks with space for two bikes on #20 and #40 buses, all hours. If rack is full, bikes allowed inside, behind the rear door, on a space available basis, with front wheel removed. For information call (707) 422–BUSS.
Golden Gate Transit Buses	Two bikes allowed inside in the wheelchair area on a space available basis only, on selected routes. Route 40, all hours; routes 60, 70, 80, within time restrictions. Cyclists must yield to wheelchair passengers. Bring a bungee cord to secure bike. For information in San Francisco call (415) 923–2000; in Marin (415) 455–2000; in Sonoma (707) 541–2000.
Golden Gate Transit Ferries	Bikes allowed on a first-come, first-serve basis; up to twenty-five bikes can be accommodated. For information in San Francisco call (415) 923–2000; in Marin (415) 455–2000; in Sonoma (707) 541–2000.
Muni	Exterior racks with space for two bikes on the following lines, all hours: 17, 35, 36, 37, 39, 53, 56, 66, 76, and 91 Owl (which operates 1:00 to 5:00 A.M.). For information call (415) 673–MUNI.
Napa Valley Transit	Exterior racks with space for two bikes on all buses, all hours. Up to two bikes allowed inside on a space available basis. For information call (800) 696–6443.
Petaluma Transit	Two bikes allowed inside bus on a space available basis, all hours. Bikes must yield to disabled persons. Cyclists who relinquish space on bus will be given a free ticket. For information call (707) 778–4460.
SamTrans	Two bikes allowed inside bus, providing bus is less than 50 percent full, all hours. Bicyclists must be age sixteen or older. Cyclists must yield to wheelchair passengers. For information call (800) 660–4287.
Santa Clara Valley Transportation Authority	Exterior racks with space for two bikes on all buses, all hours. Up to four bikes allowed inside Light Rail Cars, all hours. For information call (408) 817–1717 or (408) 321–2300.

Information

Agency	Information
Sonoma County Transit	Exterior racks with space for two bikes on intercity routes during daytime hours. After dark, up to two bikes can be taken on bus. For information call (707) 576–7433.
Tri Delta Transit	Exterior racks with space for two bikes on all buses, all hours. Bikes may also be allowed inside bus on a space available basis. For information call (925) 754–4040.
Union City Transit	Up to two bikes allowed inside on a space available basis, all hours. Bikes must be kept out of aisle. For information call (510) 471–1411.
Vacaville City Coach	Exterior racks with space for two bikes on all buses, all hours. For information call (707) 449–6000.
Vallejo Bay Link Ferry	Bikes allowed on a first-come, first-serve basis; up to twenty bicycles can be accommodated. For information call (707) 643–3779.
Vallejo Transit	Exterior racks with space for two bikes on all buses, all hours. If racks are full, bikes allowed in rear of bus, on a space available basis. For information call (800) 640–2877.
V.I.N.E. (City of Napa)	Exterior racks with space for two bikes on all buses, all hours. Bikes allowed inside on a space available basis. For information call (800) 696–6443.
WestCAT	Exterior racks with space for two bikes on new buses, all hours. Up to two bikes allowed inside older buses without racks. For information call (510) 724–7993.
Wheels (Livermore Amador Valley Transit Authority)	Exterior racks with space for two bikes on all buses, all hours. Bikes are allowed inside on a space available basis. For information call (925) 455–7500.

Regional Transit Information

Highway 17 Express/Discovery Charter (Santa Clara Transit/Santa Cruz Transit partnership) Operates between San Jose CalTrain station and Santa Cruz. Carries two bikes per bus on front rack, all hours. For information call (408) 633–2877.

Santa Cruz Metropolitan Transit District Carries two bikes per bus on front-loading rack only. Racks are available on almost all buses. For information call (408) 425–8951.